University of Cambridge Department of Applied Economics

OCCASIONAL PAPER 49

THE STATE AND ECONOMIC DEVELOPMENT: PERU SINCE 1968

To D.J.L.F.

The State and Economic Development: Peru since 1968

E.V.K. FITZGERALD

CAMBRIDGE UNIVERSITY PRESS
CAMBRIDGE
LONDON – NEW YORK – MELBOURNE

Published by the Syndics of the Cambridge University Press
The Pitt Building, Trumpington Street, Cambridge CB2 1RP
Bentley House, 200 Euston Road, London NW1 2DB
32 East 57th Street, New York, NY 10022, USA
296 Beaconsfield Parade, Middle Park, Melbourne 3206, Australia

Library of Congress catalogue card number: 75-30443

ISBN 0 521 21141 7 hard covers
ISBN 0 521 29054 6 paperback

First published 1976

Printed in Great Britain at the University Printing House, Cambridge
(Euan Phillips, University Printer)

Contents

Tables

Preface

This book is concerned with the political economy of Peru between 1960 and 1975, and particularly with the way in which the state has intervened in the process of surplus mobilisation and allocation since 1968. It does not, therefore cover political events as such, although it does provide a framework for these, but is rather an attempt to understand the nature of the problems faced by the Peruvian planners and evaluate the resulting development strategy.

It is hoped that this exposition of the Peruvian experience since 1968, by indicating both the advantages and limitations of determined state intervention within a dependent economy, may have some implications for the underdeveloped world as a whole. In particular, the advantages to be gained from the state replacing a weak domestic capitalist class, and the difficulties of this 'development path' within a dual production structure, have implications far beyond Peru itself.

I visited Peru briefly in 1972, and returned to work with the National Planning Commission (Instituto Nacional de Planificación) for an extended period in 1974. On both occasions this was financed by the ESCOR funds of the British Ministry of Overseas Development and sponsored by the Overseas Studies Committee, Cambridge. Although, in the course of my work in Peru, I have had access to confidential data, none of this has been used in this study – although it hoped that the analysis has benefitted from a more informed viewpoint in consequence.

In particular, therefore, I would like to thank the Minister (General Loayza), Technical Director (Dr. Velasco), coordinators and staff of the INP for their unfailing help and hospitality. Also, in Peru, my thanks are due to the staffs of the Central Reserve Bank, the Ministries of Agriculture, Finance and Industry as well as the economics faculties of the Catholic, San Marcos and Pacific Universities in Lima. In England, I am indebted to the following for valuable comments on earlier drafts of this book: Geoffrey Bertram, Rosemary Thorp, Brian van Arkadie, Colin Harding and members of my Peru Seminar at the Centre of Latin American Studies, Cambridge. None of these, above all the ODM and INP, are responsible for the opinions expressed or errors contained in the study, which remain the author's own.

St. Edmund's House
Cambridge
July, 1975

E.V.K. Fitzgerald

1

Introduction

1.1 The Nature of the Study

On 3rd October 1968, the 'Gobierno Revolucionario de la Fuerza Armada' took over the Peruvian state, with the intention of reducing dependence upon foreign capital, carrying through a radical land reform, and achieving a rapid rate of economic development based on export-led industrialization. This study is concerned, then, with the policy options open to such a nationalist, reforming regime within a dependent developing economy, without committing itself to a full-fledged 'transition to socialism'.

Peru has an export-based dual economy: the dynamic factor in the modern sector is primary-export production, which provides the surplus from which the demand for modern industry and service sectors is derived, accounting for the bulk of output, but only including a minority of the workforce. The 'traditional' sector includes the peasant food-production sector, artisans and petty services, creating a low-income majority labour group, which although it does not have the capitalist relations of the modern sector, is closely dependent upon it. The economy as a whole has grown steadily fairly over the past fifteen years, although the degree of real 'development' is difficult to assess, because the distribution of income has remained highly skewed, the rate of private capital accumulation has declined, the extent of industrialization has been limited and food agriculture has grown less rapidly than population.

The main contradiction was, however, not the structural difficulties in the economy but the issue of the ownership of the means of production because by 1968, the major economic sectors were dominated by a combination of foreign and domestic monopoly capital – and particularly since the penetration of foreign capital had deepended during the preceding decade to the extent of virtually reducing the role of domestic large capital to that of rentier. Thus, the main political issues were foreign domination of the export sector, the structure of land tenure, and the concentration of power in finance and industry. These did, of course, have serious consequences for the nature of economic development in Peru (such as slow employment expansion, regional disequilibrium, lack of intersectoral integration and food shortages), but it was the extent of foreign and 'oligarchic' ownership which formed the central political issue.

The reforms carried out since 1968 have been mostly concerned, therefore with the structure of ownership. First, a number of key foreign enterprises have passed into the public sector, including oil, mining, banking, fishing and communications. Second, a radical land reform has been implemented, transforming all the large estates into workers' cooperatives. Third, the state sector has been extended in scope and size – covering basic industry, most exports, banking and food marketing. Fourth, some forms of worker participation have been introduced into production enterprises involving shares in both profits and equity for modern sector labour. The effect of these reforms has been twofold. On the one hand the state has substantially replaced domestic capitalists as the 'national entrepreneur', taking over not only the responsibility of organizing production and accumulating capital, but also the relationships with foreign enterprise and domestic labour. On the other, the reforms have been limited to the ownership of the means of production in the modern sector, and thus benefit only a quarter of the workforce, the rest, particularly those in the traditional sector having been unaffected by the 'revolution'.

It is within this dual economic structure and reformed ownership system that the activities of the state must be analysed. The new role for the state has led to a considerable improvement in the planning system, and the rate of capital formation has been raised again, while investment is being redirected towards industry, but the continued lack of response from domestic capital has lead to steady expansion of the state in order to achieve specific policy objectives. Domestic economic policy since 1968 was one of stabilization, while negotiations with foreign capital have been dominated by the need to renegotiate the external debt and secure foreign capital cooperation for two key projects (oil and copper) on the one hand, and the desire to reduce external dependency on the other. This somewhat contradictory position has lead to a serious problem in public finance, however, as the state does not command sufficient control over the surplus to finance its increased burden of capital formation. Nor, indeed, does it control domestic manufacturing to the extent necessary for direct output planning.

This situation represents a considerable step forward in the development of the Peruvian political economy, but presents two major problems to be resolved. First, the underlying duality of the economy has been unaffected by the reforms, so that the accompanying difficulties of narrow domestic markets, inequitable income distribution and inadequate food supplies remain. Second, the difficulty of securing adequate public finance has lead to excessive reliance on external borrowing and inflationary domestic finance. The resolution of these problems is interconnected and in the long run further reforms will probably be necessary if Peru is not to slip back into dependent capitalist underdevelopment.

Insofar as the object of the military intervention has been to remedy the failure of the domestic capitalist elite to modernize the structure of ownership, negotiate adequately with foreign capital, rationalize the structure of production, raise the rate of investment and generally 'develop' the country, the achievements of the military regime and its plans for the future must also be assessed in these terms. As this study attempts to show, the progress so far, for all its shortcomings, does represent an important example of how a small dependent export economy can achieve a substantially greater degree of autonomous economic development by determined state intervention in the economy. Both the successes and contradiction of this process have important implications for other developing countries intending to follow a similar path.

1.2 The State in Latinamerican Development

It might be useful to make some comments upon the general position of the state in the Latinamerican political economy, so as to place the Peruvian experience in a relevant context. This inevitably involves a dangerous degree of generalization, but there is enough in common between the eighteen republics to enable us to draw some relevant conclusions.[1]

There is a long history of state intervention in the Latinamerican economies, rooted in a bureaucratic tradition established under the Spanish Crown, and involving reliance of the domestic capitalist on manipulation of government controls (such as import tariffs and mining concessions) and the provision of public sector support (such as roads or underwriting for loans) to a greater extent than in the European economies of the time. This relationship was established in the context of primary export economies, where much of the production and trade was controlled by foreign capital – initially British but after the turn of the century increasingly from the United States, while the state provided physical infrastructure and raised loans on metropolitan markets to finance it.[2]

The collapse of the metropolitan economies in the 1930's had serious repercussions on the peripheral economies, reducing both the dynamic effect of export demand and the supply of imported manufactures, forcing the Latinamerican economies in upon themselves. This engendered a certain degree of autonomous industrialization, particularly in the larger economies, based upon import-substitution but constrained by narrow domestic markets. The state began to play a more active role, providing general infrastructure (such as electric power) and development finance (the 'bancos de fomento') to the private sector, a process which continued after the Second War, with a renewed participation of the multinational corporations in the private sector and the 'aid' agencies in the public. The Latinamerican economies as a whole, however, still suffer from excessive dependence on what are essentially slow-growing export markets and narrow domestic markets, due to the maldistribution of income. The resolution of this contradiction involves a number of (possibly temporary) solutions, including the search for common customs unions, the generation of internal demand by expanding middle-class consumption, and state intervention.[3] However, far from this contradiction leading to a collapse of dependent capitalism, as had been anticipated at the beginning of the 1960's, the state has come to take an important part in the process of capital formation and economic activity.[4]

The state can intervene in the economy in two ways, either to support dependent capitalist development or to control the economy.[5] In the former case, the state supports the transfer of the surplus to the capitalist, both indirectly by maintaining the system of surplus extraction (e.g. by restraining real wages) or directly by subsidies through public enterprise and provision of infrastructure, responding to the requirements of domestic and foreign enterprise. In the latter case, the state controls the economy (or at least the modern sector) and thus can allocate the surplus itself. This might occur in various forms, depending upon the political composition of the state itself, and here we might distinguish three possibilities: first, where the state controls the economy in the interests of domestic and foreign capital, thus becoming an extreme form of the support case, acting as a 'committee of the bourgeoisie' in the conventional marxian interpretation of fascism; second, the other extreme, where the state takes over the means of production as part of an explicit transition to socialism, with state power in the hands (at least nominally) of the masses. Brazil and Cuba, respectively, might well be cited as examples. Thirdly, an intermediate stage is possible, where the state intervenes to replace the domestic bourgeoisie, with a certain degree of class-autonomy but in the process being of most benefit to the middle class and organized labour. This has been defined by Kalecki[6] as an 'intermediate regime', and possible cases outside Latin America might be Egypt and India.

The specific 'public sector' activities of public finance and development planning reflect these changing roles.[7] Generally, the Latinamerican tax system is weak, relying upon indirect taxation on external trade and consumption, rather than direct pressure on profits or high personal incomes. The pressure to expand current expenditure on health, education and defence (partly due to the need to create white-collar employment) means that most Latinamerican governments must finance capital expenditure out of inflationary domestic borrowing, fiduciary emission or external debt. This last places the state in a weak position with respect to foreign capital, which is increasingly favouring joint enterprise with the state itself.[8] Although economic planning in Latinamerica is over a decade old, it is directed towards securing external finance rather than as part of a decision mechanism. This arises, quite logically, from the support role of the state, which permits the government neither control over production decisions in the economy, nor acquisition of an adequate share of the surplus – both necessary conditions for effective planning.

It is against this background that the Peruvian experience must be seen. Clearly, by the standards of, say, Argentina, Brazil or Mexico, Peru is a 'latecomer' to economic development and thus started in 1968 from a limited scale of state intervention, but whether the new Peruvian model is indeed a 'new road to development', or merely an accelerated means of 'catching up', remains to be seen.

1.3 The Political Background

It is necessary to examine briefly the political background of the recent past in Peru, particularly since these events are not the prime concern of the study itself, although the analysis of the political economy does provide a framework within which they may be understood.

Since achieving independence from Spain early in the nineteenth century, Peru had been effectively ruled by an export-based oligarchy[9] organized in large capitalist units and dependent upon close relations with foreign capital, while relying upon the military to suppress popular movements, and take power temporarily in times of crisis. The particular expression of populism in the 1930's and early 40's was the APRA party, based on the original proletarian class formations in the mechanized sugar estates and the growing urban masses.[10] In the late 1940's, however, the APRA achieved a compromise relationship with the oligarchy, and particularly with foreign capital, while in the 1950's foreign penetration deepened the mining sector. Meanwhile, however, the post-war professionalization of the military and the increasingly explicit dependence of domestic upon foreign capital led to an awareness on the part of the officer corps of their subservient role in the maintenance of the status quo.[11]

In 1962, on the occasion of elections in which the APRA would have emerged the dominant party, the military intervened in the first 'modern' Peruvian coup. It is here, indeed, that the roots of the 1968 intervention are to be found, as the 1957–62 government of Prado and Beltran had been the last of the old oligarchic regimes.[12] Intervention of this type, in order to 'defend the constitution' is foreseen in the constitution, but this was the first where the military can be said to have acted as a relatively autonomous force. Their 'professionalism' can partly traced to the influence of the 'Centro de Altos Estudios Militares', an elite military training school established in 1951 to provide instruction in modern 'peacekeeping' but which involved the participants becoming aware of the social problems in the country – particularly foreign ownership and land tenure.[13] The changing class structure in the country as a whole, moreover, with the emergence of a 'middle class' of bureaucrats, corporate administrators, professionals and small entrepreneurs as a political force (albeit an inchoate one) was clearly important as well. On that occasion, however, the military remained in power for a short period, installing Belaunde as president in 1963, with the support of the emergent middle class and some sections of domestic and foreign capital, to pursue a specifically reformist, although gradualist, programme involving land reform and firmer negotiation with foreign capital.

This solution did not turn out to be viable. The pressure for real land reform led to land invasions and guerilla warfare in the middle of the decade, and although the latter was successfully suppressed by the military, it had a profound influence upon the officer corps. In the 1966–67 period, the economy ran into a disequilibrium, made up of a large fiscal deficit, caused by parliamentary pressure for increased public expenditure but refusal to vote tax increases, and a balance of payments deficit caused by imports rising faster than exports.[14] This crisis required severe deflationary measures and devaluation of the sol, the effects of which were most evident in 1968. The major issue during that year was, however, the negotiations between the government and the International Petroleum Company over the legal status of that company's concessions.[15] Throughout the decade, popular pressures against foreign capital had been growing, while at the same time foreign penetration (particularly that of multinationals in import-substituting consumer durables and banking) was deepening, financed by domestic capital. But, it was this particular issue, which had a long political history, that convinced the military that direct intervention was necessary.

On October 3, 1968, a group of senior military officers took over the state,[16] suspended democratic institutions, exiled the president and a few leading right-wing politicians and announced their intention of expropriating the assets of IPC, carrying through an effective land reform and achieving autonomous economic development. Their leader and commander-in-chief, General Juan Velasco Alvarado, became president, supported by a remarkable degree of solidarity within the military. This leadership and cohesion has been sustained since that date, although there have been some signs of alarm in the navy at the rate of reform on the one hand, and pressure from a 'radical' group of younger generals for further progress on the other. The changing balance between these forces has led to some changes in direction, but the overall strategy has been steadily maintained. This is not to say, however, that the military had forseen all the reforms that were eventually undertaken – on the contrary, it would appear that they had only anticipated the expropriation of IPC and the land reform, and that the subsequent reforms have been the result of responses to difficulties in implementing certain policy decisions. In particular, the incapacity of domestic capital to modernize the economy has had much to do with the massive extension of state intervention.[17]

Without anticipating the analytical conclusions of Chapter 7, the best description of the 'Peruvian model' would appear to be Kalecki's concept of an 'intermediate regime',[18] with a dominant state sector, but neither in support of domestic and foreign capital, as in the case of Brazil, nor as part of an explicitly socialist system, as in Cuba. It would appear, moreover, that the Peruvian state is to some extent independent of the domestic class structure, but that the main source of support is the 'middle classes' referred to above and those sections of organized labour that have benefited from the reforms. The circumstances that permitted the emergence of such a regime are, naturally, also those that generate the political constraints upon the policy options open to the government, and this must be borne in mind in the analysis that follows. Finally, the Revolutionary Government of the Armed Forces' own definition of the national objectives runs as follows:

> "The National Objectives are identified in terms of three permanent propositions which translate the historical and political aspirations and interests of the Nation. These National Objectives are:
>
> Establishment of a more just society, without privilege, free of marginalisation and economic, social, political or cultural discrimination, so as to provide growing possibilities for a full and integrated development of human capacity based upon common action and the security of an authentic national culture.
>
> Accelerated and self-sustaining economic development, fundamentally of the internal potential of the country, through an articulated and integrated productive structure, in both sectoral and regional terms, characterized by a substantial increase in the domestic product, a greater degree of efficiency in the use of human and natural resources and a greater rationality in the occupation of the national territory.
>
> Full exercise of national sovreignty, in both the internal and external fields, guaranteeing national control over domestic resources, securing the integrity of the territory, executing an autonomous external policy and using the complementary contribution of the external sector to national development." (INP (1971), repeated in PRP (1974) – author's translation).

1.4 Layout of the Text

The text is broadly divided into three parts. The first covers the organization of the present political economy of Peru, including the structure of the economy itself (Chapter 2) and the reforms carried out since 1968 (Chapter 3). The second part is concerned with the economic role of the state within this structure, covering the organization of the state itself in this respect (Chapter 4), economic policy (Chapter 5) and development planning (Chapter 6). Finally, the third part consists in an attempt to assess the implications of the study as a whole, including an analysis of the present system and strategy for the future (Chapter 7).

Although the study includes a brief summary of the available data sources (Appendix IV), it would not be otiose to mention the matter here also. There is an extraordinary paucity of published studies of the Peruvian economy, and indeed there is no known book, of any substance in Spanish or English on the subject as a whole. Nor does there exist a substantial economic history, although the forthcoming work by Thorp and Bertram covering the period since 1890 will be of great value to scholars in the field. The consequence for this study is double; on the one hand, there is more space dedicated to description of the economy than might otherwise be necessary, and on the other this description is bound to be inadequate. The consequences of this deficiency will be noted in the text below.

The final manuscript for this book was completed in the summer of 1975, and thus can only take into account events up to the spring of that year – it is hoped that the conclusions have not been overtaken by history in the interim.*

NOTES TO CHAPTER 1

1. Fitzgerald (1974)
2. Sunkel & Paz (1971)
3. Furtado (1970)
4. ECLA (1971)
5. Sachs (1964)
6. Kalecki (1972 b)
7. Cibotti & Sierra (1970)
8. As ECLA (1971) points out:

   The traditional idea of conflict between the public and private sectors ceases to have any meaning in many cases . . . (because) . . . the real choice is between public and semi-public enterprises and foreign or international enterprises. At the same time . . . the existence of the state enterprise sector has definitely had the effect of helping the private sector to extend its operations".
9. See Levin (1960) and Pike (1967). The Peruvian Republic is no stranger to military rule – during the period 1821–1968 50 out of 76 presidents were military, ruling for 86 years out of the 147.
10. See Payne (1965)
11. Villanueva (1971)
12. Astiz (1969)
13. Villanueva (1971)
14. See Chapter 2.7
15. Pinelo (1973)
16. Zimmerman (1974) who is, incidentally, the press secretary to the presidency, and gives an 'insider's view'.
17. Conflicting views are given by Quijano (1971) against, and Delgado (1972) for.
18. Kalecki (1972 b).

* In August 1975, Persident Velasco was replaced by the former prime minister (previously chief of staff, and earlier finance minister), General Francisco Morales Bermudez. This 'institutional succession' does not appear to mean, however, any fundamental change in strategy.

2

The Political Economy

2.1 General

In order to understand the problems of the Peruvian economy today, it is necessary to examine its roots. These lie, naturally, in the past, and although they stretch back centuries, we shall confine ourselves to the background contained in the last fifteen years as a whole.

The general ecology of Peru is not described here[1] but the main features are as follows. The population totals some 14 million, of original Amerindian descent (predominating in rural areas) and immigrants of European, African and Asian origin, having mainly arrived as colonists, slaves and indentured labour respectively. The landmass is divided into Costa (desert Pacific coast), Sierra (somewhat barren Andes mountains) and Selva (Amazonian rain forest), covering an extremely wide range of ecological zones. There is relatively little arable land but rich mineral deposits, particularly metals and oil. The capital is Lima, there being few provincial cities of any size, and a steady migratory movement towards the coast.

In this chapter, we set out to show the political economy fits together in terms of the structure of production, overseas trade, income distribution and the ownership of the means of production on the one hand, and the rate of capital accumulation and output growth on the other. It is argued here that the economy has a dual structure, separating the export-led, capital-intensive modern sector from the labour-intensive, low-income traditional sector, although the two are interdependent. The nature of economic development in this form of dependent capitalism has been such as to generate a distorted production system, with a primary export sector dominating the economy, an externally linked industrial and financial system, and a highly skewed distribution of personal income. The pattern of ownership in 1968 was, so to speak, the other side of the same coin, and underlay the political structure. There was a high degree of concentration exhibited in land tenure, industrial property and financial control, the whole closely linked with foreign capital. The growth record of the decade had been one of deceleration, leading to the 1966–67 disequilibrium, and although the rate of output expansion revived subsequently, the rate of capital formation remained low. It is argued in this chapter, however, that the problems of the Peruvian economy are basically due to the existence of this duality and lack of the coordination necessary to resolve it, although in its day-to-day functioning the aggregate economy exhibits a remarkable stability.

At this stage it might be useful to attempt a summary definition of three terms that we have already used and will be employed quite frequently below. First *duality*. By this we do not mean the dichotomy between an industrial, urban, capitalist 'modern sector' on the one hand and an agricultural, rural, peasant 'traditional sector' on the other, without any relationship between them, in the sense indicated by Lewis or Fei & Ranis.[2] On the contrary, it is clear that both in Latin America as a whole and particularly in Peru, the capitalist system has penetrated deeply into the entire economy. What we do mean here by duality is the situation where a section of the economy (a sub-sector of primary, secondary and tertiary production sectors) is more highly capitalised than the rest, acquiring both by higher physical productivity and by internal terms of trade, the bulk of the national product while employing a minority of the workforce. It is here that the middle and upper classes are rooted, while maintaining close relationships with the traditional sector, manifested in the supply of labour and wagegoods on the one hand, and the demand for petty services and 'putting out' of parts of the production process on the other. The concept of duality, as will be seen, is essential to an understanding of the nature of the Peruvian political economy. Other titles, such as 'corporate'/'household', or 'formal'/'informal' might be used, but 'moderno/tradicional' is the terminology used by Peruvian social scientists, and as long as it is used with caution, appears to be the most useful.

Second *surplus*. Here we use this word in the sense indicated by Baran[3] of the excess of material production over the basic consumption requirements of the workforce. This is an important concept, as the extraction of this surplus from the producers, and its allocation between uses such as investment, capitalist consumption, middle-class income and government expenditure is the basis of the political economy. However, it is notoriously difficult to pin down in quantitative terms, as so much depends upon the definition of 'basic consumption requirements'. At best we can estimate the bounds within which the value must lie: the lower bound would be total saving plus government consumption, while the upper bound would be total output less the multiple of the population and the per capita consumption of the lower income strata. In the Peruvian case, this would mean a figure of between one and two thirds of output,[4] so in the spirit of compromise, we might set the 'disposable surplus' as one-half of output. The exact figure is not crucial to the analysis, but it is useful to have some idea of the relationship between the surplus actually realized, particularly in terms of investment and state expenditure and its potential level.

Third, *dependency*. Here we use this much-abused term in the sense employed by Baran (1957), Furtado (1970) and Sunkel & Paz (1971), so as to indicate a situation where a considerable degree of economic control is subordinated to foreign decision centres. Clearly this occurs in any economy to a certain extent, but in this sense it is understood to refer to the underdeveloped 'periphery' economies in relation to the capitalist 'metropolitan' nations. Four aspects of economic dependence can be distinguished: first, the ownership by foreign forms of the domestic means of production; second, the 'export' of the domestically generated surplus in the form of profits and transfers; third, the control over technology, particularly in the form of capital goods and manufacturing patents; and last, the control over sources of international finance, particularly official loans. The pattern of dependency as a whole is reflected in the close connexion of the domestic capital to foreign enterprise, the reliance upon primary goods exports, and a lack of autonomous capacity for capital formation – that is, an independent capital goods sector. Further, to these should be added a phenomenon known as 'cultural dependency' which although difficult to define is clearly important, as it is a crucial factor in the determination of a distorted consumption structure which itself requires a certain foreign technology to satisfy it, thus reinforcing the dependent relationship.

2.2 The Structure of Output

The structure of economic production underlies the pattern of ownership, the social structure and the political system. In the Peruvian case, however, the production structure is similar in 1975 to what it was in 1960, and it is within this structure that the changes have been made. The essential feature of the production system are its duality, its export-led dynamics, and its 'under-development' in the sense of a small and disarticulated industrial base, as well as a low level of output per head. The historical roots of the present are almost a paradigm of the dependent export economy,[5] the centuries of 'desarollo hacia afuera' having led to an economy where the focus of domestic and foreign capital is the primary export sector, developing trading and finance activities in support, while industry is based on the narrow import-substitution market and food agriculture is neglected. We cannot, of course, describe the economy in adequate detail,[6] but a brief survey would be useful. We shall proceed by considering the sectors separately, and then explore the dynamics of the present system.

Agriculture[7] occupies nearly half the workforce, but accounts for less than a fifth of the national output. In product terms, the sector can be conveniently divided between industrial crops (sugar, cotton on the coast, wool in the mountains) and foodcrops (maize, potatoes, rice etc.), these being respectively organised in large capitalized estates and peasant farms. However, of the 1.29 million square kilometers of national territory, only 0.30 is agricultural land, and of this a mere 0.03 is arable, the rest being poor mountain pasture.[8] It would appear that much of the best land is in the coastal areas under export enterprises, and the pattern is repeated in the sierra, the small remainder being in peasant hands.[9] In consequence, about a quarter of the agricultural labour force is permanently employed on estates, with another 15% coming in as seasonal labour from both rural towns and peasant agriculture. Production on the large estates is highly organized and integrated into processing and exports, with good access to finance and inputs. Food production, in contrast, is technically backward, poorly organized and lacking in finance and inputs.

Minerals[10] form the keystone of the export sector. The Andes mountains contain considerable amounts of copper, lead, zinc, iron and silver, many of them exploited from pre-colombian times, while the northern coast and Amazonian region hold oil. The mines are primarily exploited by large corporations, as is the case with oil – the coastal deposits of this latter having been exhausted, large new reserves are being opened up in the jungle. The sector is a relatively small employer of labour, although it is a significant 'educator' of skilled labour, but is an important generator of foreign exchange and surplus in the form of profits and taxation. The third element of the primary sector is fishing, which is dominated by the fishmeal industry (for animal feed), based on the exploitation of the Pacific anchovy. This has created, over the past two decades, a large fleet and processing plant, making Peru the largest producer in the world[11].

Industry in Peru is relatively underdeveloped. Of manufacturing output, about a quarter is concerned with processing export products (minerals, sugar, fishmeal) and about half is in traditional consumer goods (food processing, textiles etc) and the remaining quarter in basic support industry (steel, cement, fertilizers etc.)[12]. A process of import substitution has been under way for two decades but this has involved the 'typical' multinational assembly plants within tariff barriers,[13] and there is, in consequence, no true capital goods sector.[14] Manufacturing is sharply divided between large capitalist enterprise, which accounts for about two thirds of output, and artisan production (i.e. in firms of five or less) which accounts for about two thirds of the workforce. Industry as a whole is not intersectorally integrated, and thus extremely dependent upon imported materials and capital goods.[15] The construction sector has grown rapidly in response to the urban expansion since the second world war and is an important source of profit and employer of unskilled labour.

In the tertiary sector (omitting government, which is the subject of Chapter 4) we find the dual pattern repeated. The financial sector is highly concentrated and relatively sophisticated[16], due principally to its role in linking oligopolic enterprises in different sectors and transferring funds between them. Commerce, like manufacturing, is divided sharply between large wholesale and retail stores on the one hand, which employ only a minority of the workforce, and a mass of petty traders, small bars and so on[17], on the other. In transport (which suffers, incidentally, from a poor road network) and services the same pattern emerges, especially in the latter – within which nearly half the workforce is in domestic service.

Table 1 shows the overall pattern that emerges, and the stable structure of the economy should be noted, within which a secular decline of the relative position of agriculture and rise in that of services is taking place.

The diversified primary export sector is the prime mover of economic activity, both directly as part of the production process and indirectly as a generator of investable profits, tax revenue and consumption demand as well as being the main supplier of foreign exchange. The gross value of exports is equivalent to one-fifth of GNP, and when processing is included, the value added in their production accounts for one-seventh of GNP – about one quarter of modern sector output, making it larger than the non-export sections of either agriculture or manufacturing. This motive force of the economy has been gradually complemented by the endogenous growth factors of domestic industry and the public sector, but is itself largely exogenous – being based on world markets and natural resource availability. This dynamic feeds through to the manufacturing and construction sectors, not by means of input linkages[18] but rather by the generation of expendible surplus, through a highly concentrated income distribution, supported by the financial system and imported technology. Dependent upon this modern sector for markets, but excluded from the income benefits, are food agriculture and petty services, the former, in particular, having grown very slowly. The allocation of the labour force reflects the requirements of this system; relatively little labour (relative to the share of production) is needed in the modern sector, which is reasonably technically advanced and capital-intensive – roughly a third of the total. This leaves the rest of the economically active population to be distributed between traditional agriculture and the urban tertiary sector, with internal migration taking place[19] away from

Table 1. Structure of Production in the Peruvian Economy: 1960–72

	GNP at 1963 Prices (%)				Workforce (%)			
	1960	1964	1968	1972	1960	1964	1968	1972
Agriculture & Fishing	22.4	20.0	17.2	14.0	52.3	49.6	48.4	45.9
Mining	7.2	6.1	6.0	4.7	2.2	2.1	2.2	2.2
Manufacturing	17.3	18.8	21.2	22.0	13.3	14.0	14.1	14.4
Construction	4.2	4.0	3.2	3.9	3.2	3.7	3.9	4.2
Government	7.8	8.2	8.6	8.2	5.3	5.6	6.7	7.3
Other	41.0	42.9	43.5	47.3	23.7	25.0	24.7	26.0
Totals (soles bn)	64.2	84.1	95.4	130.1				
millions					3.16	3.55	3.93	4.37
soles '000/head	20.3	23.7	24.3	29.8				

Source: Compiled from BCR (1974a) and BCR (1967)

rural areas towards the towns in response to the demand for petty services generated by the modern sector. Overall, then, the growth of the modern sector, even though it does not generate much employment itself, does lead to urban migration, which is reinforced by the slow expansion of peasant agriculture – resulting in growing sectoral imbalance and a chronic food supply problem.

In an attempt to fit this dual structure together in a way distinct from the conventional national accounts definition given above, table 2 (from Appendix II) shows the allocation of output and labour between the modern and traditional sectors, and although the ratio of these cannot be directly used as a measure of 'productivity'[20], the overall ratio of value-added per worker in the modern sector to the traditional is nearly three to one.

Table 2. Structure of Output (1972)

	% Value Added	% Workforce
Modern		
Export Production	19	18
Industry	11	5
Government & Tertiary	31	13
	61	36
Traditional		
Food Agriculture	10	33
Small Industry	9	11
Petty Tertiary	20	20
	39	64

Source: Appendix II

2.3 The External Sector

The balance of payments is the external manifestation of the production structure outlined above, and above all of the outward orientation of the economy – exporting primary and import dependent secondary sectors. The distinguishing characteristics are the diversity of the primary export structure and the import-substitution process, combined with the growing importance of food imports. The resulting trade balance exhibits considerable stability, although a sharp disequilibrium was experienced in the middle of the period under consideration. Capital account reflects the structure of capital accumulation, and is not discussed here but in the penultimate section of this chapter.

Exports are almost entirely[21] primary processed products, principally minerals (copper, zinc, iron, lead, silver etc.), fishmeal and fish-oil, and agroproducts (sugar, cotton, wool, coffee), which provide a diversified export base, although the product composition has varied quite markedly over time within these groups.[22] The other main characteristic is their steady growth over time, which is due as much to changes in world prices as it is to expanded volume.

Imports are mainly composed of the inputs for the modern sector industries,

Table 3. Peruvian Exports: 1960–72

% Current Value (FOB)	1960	1964	1968	1972
Minerals, Oil	49	40	51	46
Agroproducts	33	31	19	20
Fishmeal	11	25	27	23
Others	7	4	3	11
$US value (mn)	433	667	866	943
Unit value index	100	129	119	131

Source: BCR (1974a), BCR (1967), ONEC (1973)

there having occurred over the past two decades a process of partial import-substitution[23], leading to reduced imports of consumer goods, balanced by increased food imports. The capital goods item represents virtually the entire supply of machinery and equipment to the economy. The sharp fall in unit value is due to consumer durables embargoes imposed in 1968.

Table 4. Peruvian Imports: 1960–72

% Current Value (CIF)	1960	1964	1968	1972
Food & Food Products	16	16	20	19
Consumer Goods	15	15	11	7
Intermediate Inputs	34	35	36	32
Capital Goods	35	34	33	42
$US value (mn)	375	580	630	797
Unit value index	100	115	97	99

Source: as previous table.

Combining these to give the visible trade balance, and adding the services transactions yields the current account, shown in table 5 and expressed in relation to the GDP. The effects of the growth of the domestic economy can be seen in the declining ratio of trade to total output, as can the effects of the excessive expansion of domestic demand in the middle of the period, which required devaluation in 1967 and import restrictions to stabilize the economy.

The exchange rate over the medium term reflects the relative rate of inflation in domestic and international markets, and as the rate of price rise has not been excessive in Peru, the only significant change in the exchange rate in the period since 1960 has been the devaluation from 27 to 43 soles to the US dollar at the end of 1967. The main effect of such changes is upon imports, as the export sectors are dependent on world markets and natural resource availability and respond to external rather than internal prices.

Finally, the direction of trade, once again, reflects the internal structure of production and the external dependency of the economy. The outstanding features, as

Table 5. Balance of Payments: 1960–74. (%GDP)

	1960–64	1965–68	1969–72	1973–74
Exports of goods & serv.	23.0	18.9	18.3	14.7
Imports of goods & serv.	24.3	22.2	17.4	16.1
Current account Balance	−1.3	−3.3	+0.9	−1.4
Long capital flow	+0.6	+2.8	−0.4	+4.0
Short capital, monetary and transfer flows	+0.7	+0.5	−0.5	−2.6

Source: as previous table, plus BCR (1974c)

table 6 shows, are the dominant (although decreasing) share of the USA and European markets on the one hand, and the very small participation of other Latin-american economies (let alone the Andean Pact) on the other. In the main, minerals go to North America and fishmeal to Europe.

Table 6. The Direction of Peruvian Trade: 1960–73 (percent)

	1960	1964	1968	1973
Exports				
USA	36	31	39	35
Europe	37	44	44	31
Latin America	9	10	6	7
Imports				
USA	44	41	34	29
Europe	46	38	28	27
Latin America	7	11	16	10

Source: as previous table.

2.4 The Population and the Distribution of Personal Income

Here we shall examine the relevant aspects of the population structure and, derived from the production structure, the distribution of personal income. The general picture is one of fundamentally rural population, growing quite rapidly with an increasing tendency towards migration into the urban service sector. The distribution of income is based on the dual structure of the economy, which determines the low income level of the bulk of the population, and the concentration of earnings within the modern sector.

Censi were carried out in 1876, 1940, 1961 and 1972, revealing a population growth rate rising from 2.2% (1940–41) to 2.9% (1961–72) – the result above all of declining infant mortality rates[24]. The population in 1972 was 13.60 millions, of which 41% was recorded as residing in urban areas[25] compared with 28% in 1961 (a growth rate of 6.4%), the metropolitan share in 1972 being 28% of the national total. Internal migration appears to have accelerated over the past decade, but intercensal data does not permit of more precise analysis, and it would appear that migration is a 'staged' process, involving movement to rural towns and from them to the capital – so that the recent growth of urban centres other than Lima may be a transitional phenomenon. In terms of the major natural regions, the population is divided between costa (43%), sierra (47%) and selva (10%).

The economically active population (whose sectoral distribution has been analysed above) in 1972 was some 4.37 millions[26], a participation rate of 32% which reflects the youth of the growing population on the one hand (45% of the population is aged 14 or less) and the relatively high female participation rate (30% of the 15–65 age group) in agriculture and domestic service, on the other. The rapid population growth, and the still more rapid urban expansion is a considerable problem, particularly since the migrating labour is not absorbed into productive employment.

The distribution of personal income in Peru emerges logically from the duality of the economy (discussed in section 2 of this chapter) and the concentration of ownership within the modern sector (section 5), and itself is the determinant of the domestic demand structure. The low-income 'base' is made up of small peasants, landless labour, and the 'tail' of the urban service sector. As we have seen, the market value of output per head on the traditional sector is little more than a third of that in the modern sector, and within this group there are wide variations. Turning to the modern sector, we find a progressive concentration of income through 'blue-collar' and 'white-collar' workers, professionals, small and large capitalists. The functional distribution of income is not reliably estimated in Peru[27], but the recorded share of property income in national product (21% in 1972) compared with that of the modern sector (about 60%) reveals the magnitudes involved. Webb (1972 b) has made the first, and so far only, reliable estimate of income distribution, based on the 1961 census, and there is reason to believe that the position in 1968 was more or less the same.

Table 7. Personal Income Distribution

Proportion of Workforce		Share of Income	Income per head of population ($US)*
Highest	5%	39%	1560
Top	20%	65%	650
Middle	40%	26%	130
Lower	40%	9%	45

Source: based on Webb (1972b).
*Distribution applied to 1972 mean income per head.

It is difficult to gauge in absolute terms whether this is a 'bad' distribution, but the extremely low standard of living of the bulk of the population (which is, after all, integrated into the market economy at international commodity price levels) is noticeable, even by Latinamerican standards[28], and another important aspect is the relative absence of 'middle strata' in the distribution. There is also a considerable *regional* income imbalance, which reflects to a great extent the spatial concentration of the modern sector in Lima, on the northern coast and in the Andean mining enclaves. According to the 1961 economic census, the metropolis, with only 22% of the population at that date, received 43% of the national income.[29] This imbalance seems to have been steadily worsening, due to internal migration and the slow growth of peasant agriculture. Table 8 illustrates the weak position of 'agricultores independientes' (mostly heads of peasant families) whose share of national income has steadily fallen and whose absolute income appears to have scarcely risen at all over the decade.

Table 8. Peasant Incomes: 1960–72

	1960	1966	1972
% of national income	13.7	11.1	8.8
% of workforce	35.2	32.7	29.7
Ratio	.39	.34	.30
Index of real income*	100	105	102

Source: calculated from BCR (1974a). *see footnote 30.

2.5 Economic Growth

Having examined the structure of the economy for the period as a whole, and we shall now turn to the growth performance of the separate sectors since 1960[31]. Dividing the period 1960–72 into three (see table 9) we can explore the development of a growth cycle which reveals some characteristics of the dynamics of the economy that will be relevant to discussions of economic policy since 1968.

In the first period (1960–64) there was rapid export growth (particularly in fishing), which worked through to manufacturing and construction, generating a

Table 9. Average Annual Growth Rates: 1960–73
(% change at 1963 prices)

	1960–64	1965–68	1969–73	1960–73
Agriculture	3.8	−0.5	2.1	1.8
Fishing	17.1	1.5	−16.8	0.6
Mining	2.9	2.6	1.4	2.3
Manufacturing	9.2	5.3	7.1	7.2
Construction	6.4	−2.2	10.0	4.7
Services	9.2	3.8	8.9	7.3
GNP	7.6	2.9	6.3	5.6
GFCF[a]	10.3	−1.2	9.0	6.0
Prices[b]	7.4	13.7	7.3	9.5

Sources: calculated from BCR (1974a).
(a) gross fixed capital formation.
(b) GNP deflator, 1963 base.

high rate of output growth in the economy as a whole. Import growth was rapid, but below that of exports, so that the balance of payments remained stable. Agriculture grew slowly, but enough to keep pace with population growth, while inflation was kept down and the rate of capital formation was reasonably high.[32] In the second period (1965–68), however, this performance was not sustained. Export growth slowed down, as did manufacturing and the economy as a whole. Meanwhile, the pressure of internal demand (and thus import growth) was sustained by the Belaunde government leading to the balance of payments crisis and devaluation of 1967. Agricultural output was actually falling, as was the rate of capital formation, and inflation got worse. The third period (1969–73), which corresponds to the period of the reforms discussed in the next chapter, has seen a recovery of exports (in spite of the fishing collapse) and national income growth sustained by public investment, while imports have been restrained by direct controls. Agriculture has grown slower than population, however, although investment growth has revived and inflation has been moderate.[33]

The economy as a whole has made fairly steady, if not spectacular progress during the years since 1960, but the rapid rate of population growth kept down the percapita income growth and actually resulted in a fall in 1967 and 1968. It is reasonable to suppose, moreover (in the light of the discussion of section 4 of this chapter) that the personal income distribution deteriorated sharply about this time, leading to falling living standards for the mass of the populace in the years leading up to the military intervention.

Table 10. GNP per caput: 1960–73 (at 1963 prices)

	'000 soles	% change		'000 soles	% change
1960	6.34	6.1	1967	7.59	−1.4
1961	6.66	5.0	1968	7.41	−2.4
1962	7.07	6.2	1969	7.50	1.2
1963	7.12	0.7	1970	7.94	5.9
1964	7.40	3.9	1971	8.20	3.3
1965	7.50	1.4	1972	8.44	2.9
1966	7.70	2.7	1973	8.68	2.8

Source: BCR (1974a)

In particular, the relatively slow progress in industrialization is a cause for concern, and it is a stated objective of government policy to rectify this. After an initial burst in the early 1960's, based on import substitution and supplies to the fishing industry, the process slowed down. This occurred for a number of reasons[34] but the lack of markets appears to have been crucial – the end of the fishing boom and thus the input requirements, the lack of dynamism in real domestic demand (due to the concentration of personal income) after the initial substitution of consumer durables, and the failure to establish external markets for exported manufactures. The industrialization that did take place was marked by capital-intensity, little employment generation, imported inputs and penetration by multinationals.

Table 11. Growth in Manufacturing: 1960–73

	1960–64	1965–68	1969–73	1960–73
Production[a]	9.2	5.3	7.1	7.2
Employment	3.1	3.2	3.0	3.1
Productivity[b]	6.0	2.0	4.0	4.0

Source: BCR (1974a).
(a) value-added at 1963 prices
(b) production ÷ employment.

2.6 Ownership of the Means of Production

Given the essential stability of the economy, the main issue in the political economy has naturally been the ownership of the means of production, particularly in the modern sector, this pattern of ownership, in turn, conferring control over the movement of the surplus through the economy. Broadly, the 1960–68 period saw a further concentration in an already highly oligopolistic ownership system, dominated by a small number of combines closely linked to foreign capital. This phenomenon is central to this study, as it forms the background to the political economy as a whole, and to the reforms discussed in the next chapter in particular.

As a consequence of its political importance, the pattern of ownership in the late nineteensixties has received more attention than any other aspect of the political economy. In this context, the work of Malpica[35] on agriculture and foreign capital, and that of Espinosa[36] on industry, mining and fishing, are of considerable interest, but these studies are 'sociological' and do not analyse the economic functioning of the resulting structure, nor do they trace its development over time. In this section we shall examine the logic of the system, building on the output structure discussed above.

In the case of agriculture, we have already noted the extreme degree of concentration in land ownership – indeed according to the 1961 census some three-quarters of the land was under less than one percent of the units, no more than a few thousand families out of nearly a million. Three major mining companies (all US owned) have dominated the mining sector (with 75% of sales and 87% of assets in 1968)[37] for some time, while the fishing sector, although initially (1955–60) highly competitive and a breeding ground for 'indigenous entrepreneurship'[38] was rapidly concentrating (1960–65) in the hands of a few groups, themselves closely linked to foreign capital[39].

In industry,[40] this pattern is repeated, so that by 1968, the 79 largest manufacturing firms controlled about half the sales and fixed assets in manufacturing. Of these top 79 firms moreover (which only employ 15% of the workforce), only 20 were wholly nationally owned in 1968 (including 2 state enterprises) and 41 were fully foreign owned, these last accounting for 30% of capital in the manufacturing sector as a whole. The concentration of ownership and foreign penetration is spread through all the manufacturing sectors, covering both 'backward' (e.g. foodstuffs, textiles) and 'progressive' (e.g. chemicals, consumer durables) branches.

The principle source of economic power was (and is) the ownership of national resources and the financial sector, and although the domestic bourgeoisie remained

Table 12. Size Distribution in Manufacturing (1968)

<table>
<tr><th>Enterprise</th><th>% of number</th><th>% of assets</th><th>% of sales</th></tr>
<tr><td>Large</td><td>3</td><td>54</td><td>49</td></tr>
<tr><td>Medium</td><td>17</td><td>37</td><td rowspan="2">51</td></tr>
<tr><td>Small</td><td>80</td><td>9</td></tr>
</table>

Source: Espinoza (1972)

dominant, the penetration by foreign capital deepened up to 1968.[41] By this date, three quarters of mining, half of fishing, two thirds of sugar capital, and half the cotton and wool processing plant were under foreign enterprise – which gave control over perhaps two-thirds of exports. To this should be added half of commercial banking, a third of manufacturing and the ownership of key enterprises in communications, power and trade. This added up to control over a proportion of the productive assets in the modern sector of the order of between a third and a half, and over a third of all post-tax enterprise profits being exported[42]. This was achieved in conjunction with domestic capitalists, who became not only local representatives of the multinationals (as managers of affiliated companies or trademark concessionaires) but also their financiers (through the banking system) – a historical transition from capitalist to rentier. The process appears to have ocurred in two stages, the first being the original establishment of foreign control over mining and some aspects of agroindustry in the first third of the century, and second the renewed penetration in the 1955–67 period associated with fishing, import-substitution and banking. It was this foreign ownership that formed the major political issue in the years leading up to 1968, and the external dependence of domestic capital is relevant to its lack of resistance to reform after that date[43].

It was possible, in 1968, to identify six main 'ownership groups'[44] which were spread across primary, secondary and tertiary sectors. These groups controlled some 70% of sales in the 'large' industrial group in 1968 (a third of all sales in the secondary sector alone) having been originally based upon family interests in export agriculture and mining firms, but which spread out through industry into banking[45] and real estate. This granted determinate control over the mobilisation and disposition of the surplus, and moreover meant that there was no real distinction between, say, the 'industrial entrepreneur' on the one hand and the 'feudal landowner' on the other.

It is this network of ownership within the modern sector that connected the output sectors,[46] rather than technical and interindustrial ('input-output') linkages. The primary sector generated the surplus, which flowed through the banking system into the secondary sector, all within the same ownership groups. The historical roots of this[47] may well lie in the comparatively rapid changes in the 'export mix' in the past, which required domestic capital to shift frequently between sectors. The flexibility thus acquired, however, also meant that there was no particular committment to industrialisation when better investment opportunities presented themselves in other sectors.

2.7 The Accumulation of Capital

The process of accumulation takes place almost entirely in the modern sector, and is closely connected to the pattern of ownership in the economy which we have just discussed. The main features of saving in Peru are the dominance of company profits within the total and the paucity of the contribution from the public sector while on the investment side, the steadily declining rate of accumulation over time and the expansion of the state share should be noted.

In general, it would appear that the rate of private capital formation in Peru is determined by the perceived investment opportunities rather than be the availability of finance[48], while these 'opportunities' will clearly depend upon both the real state of the economy (particularly export growth and domestic demand) and the expectations of the investors themselves, particularly in reference to future political conditions and profit rates. In the public sector, investment is part of a planned process, but has been related to the private investment rate insofar as the purpose of the former is to support the latter. The corollary of this argument is that shortage of finance does not appear to have been a constraint on capital formation in Peru, and this phenomenon is important to an understanding of the Peruvian economy, as it throws light both on the decline in private investment (and the difficulty of reviving it since 1968), and on the substitution between different sources of finance and ownership – domestic and foreign capital on the one hand, and the state on the other.

Savings out of the surplus by different groups represent different means of financing capital formation, and are related to the structure of ownership in the economy. The main characteristics are shown in the table below, which demonstrates the relative unimportance of both state savings[49] (including public external borrowing) and external sources. Until 1968, this latter phenomenon was due to the ease with which foreign corporations could acquire local finance, in terms of both Peruvian currency and foreign exchange, from the Peruvian banking system. The dominant feature within the private sector is corporate saving, as personal savings have declined sharply in importance, due to two factors, both of interest in the context of the financial integration of the capitalist sector[50]. First, the emergence of 'mutuales' (building societies) in the nineteen-sixties became a dominant means of financing housebuilding and thus mortgage payments replaced personal term bank deposits used for this purpose. Second, the reform of the tax system led to the preference for retaining profits within a group rather than distributing them to shareholders for subsequent reinvestment. The accumulation system is, then, made up of a well integrated network of capitalist enterprise and financial intermediaries, which mobilise the funds and currency required for any particular rate of capital formation.

The economic cycle (see section 5 of this chapter) is reflected in the development of savings over the period not only in the declining proportion of national output accumulated, but also the fall in state savings and greater foreign finance in the second period, and the reverse position since 1968 – to the point of resulting in a net outflow of private funds abroad, mainly the outflow of amortisation funds.

We can now turn to the overall rate of capital formation. This recorded investment is essentially capital formation[51] in the modern sector, and the decline in relation to output has been further exacerbated by the rising requirements of replacement to the growing capital stock. The decline was mainly due to the deceleration of the export sector (and thus manufacturing and construction) in the

Table 13. Structure of Savings: 1960–74 (%GDP)

	1960–64	1965–68	1969–72	1973–74
Private Sector:				
Personal	7.7	1.7	1.5	14.5
Corporate	11.2	13.9	12.2	
External	0.1	1.8	−1.4	−2.0
	19.0	17.4	12.3	12.5
Public Sector	2.1	0.8	1.6	3.3
Gross Savings	21.1	18.2	13.9	14.8

Source: BCR (1974a), author's estimates.

second period, and in the third the continued weakness of private investment in the face of ownership reforms, the exclusion of foreign enterprise, and the reorganization of the public sector; although in 1973–74 the effect of state investment expansion becomes apparent.

Table 14. Capital Formation: 1960–72 (%GDP)

	1960–64	1965–68	1969–72	1973–74
Gross Savings	21.1	18.1	13.9	15.8
less Stockbuilding	2.9	2.8	1.3	1.0
gives GFCF[a]	18.2	15.3	12.6	14.8
less depreciation	5.7	6.1	6.5	6.8
gives NFCF[b]	12.5	9.2	6.1	8.0

Source: Calculated from BCR (1974a), author's estimates.
(a) Gross Fixed Capital Formation
(b) Net Fixed Capital Formation.

The system of mobilising the surplus and allocating it between the public and private sectors is a topic of some importance for other parts of our study, and it emerges naturally from the imbalance between savings and investment rates in the two sectors. Table 15 shows capital formation and savings (including foreign finance) in the two sectors, and the *net* transfer between them.[52] It also shows the steady increase in the share of the state in capital formation as a whole, rising from 20% in the first period, through 30% in the second and 39% in the third, to 49% in the fourth.

Unfortunately, very little is known about capital formation by production sector in Peru, and nothing published in aggregate sectoral form. A rough estimate[53] based on miscellaneous data for the 1965–72 period as a whole, however, would indicate that private investment is made up of approximately one-third housing, and one-fifth each in transport equipment and industry. The division between investment in machinery (i.e. plant) and construction (i.e. buildings) is significant, as the decline

Table 15. Public and Private Accumulation: 1960–74 (%GDP)

	1960–64	1965–68	1969–72	1973–74
Private Savings[a]	16.1	14.6	11.0	11.8
less Net Transfer to State	1.5	3.9	3.3	4.3
gives Private GFCF	14.6	10.7	7.7	7.5
Public Savings[a]	2.1	0.7	1.9	3.0
plus Net Transfer from Private Sector	1.5	3.9	3.3	4.3
gives Public GFCF	3.6	4.6	4.9	7.3

Source: Calculated from BCR (1974a), see also Appendix III.
(a) including foreign finance and net of stockbuilding.

in the former has been more severe than in the latter, as the table below shows. This is partly due to changes within the private sector (e.g. the urbanization process) and partly to the growth in the state (e.g. public works) share.

Table 16. Composition of Investment: 1960–72 (%GDP)

	1960–64	1965–68	1969–72
Machinery & Equipment	10.2	8.4	6.7
Construction	8.0	6.9	5.9
Total GFCF	18.2	15.3	12.6
Private Investment:			
Manufacturing	...	2.2	1.2
Transport Equipment	...	1.7	1.5
Housing	...	2.8	2.8
Other	...	4.0	2.2
	14.6	10.7	7.7

Finally, we should attempt some definition of the capitalisation of the economy as a result of this investment process. The INP has made some estimates[54], shown in the table below, which give an indication of the effect of cumulative investment (net of depreciation) in terms of the capital stock, the capital-output ratio and the capital-labour ratio for the economy as a whole. However, as the recorded capital formation only refers to the modern sector, the capital-output ratio should really be raised by one-half and the capital-labour ratio be multiplied by three. As can be seen, there has not been a great change in capitalisation per unit of output but there has been a rise in capital per head, which might be interpreted as a long-run increase in labour productivity.

2.8 Problems in the Economy

We have reviewed the political economy of Peru in those aspects relevant

Table 17. Capital Stock: 1960–71

	1960	1965	1971
Capital Stock (soles bn at 1963 prices)	184	232	288
Capital Output Ratio (at 1963 prices)	2.86	2.62	2.79
Capital Labour Ratio (soles '000 at 1963 prices)	58.5	63.7	67.7

Source: see footnote 54.

to our study, and here we shall conclude by mentioning the contradictions in the system[55]. It is against these problems, and within the structural constraints, that state intervention in the economy since 1968 must be evaluated.

We have seen how the economy, until 1968 at least, was exogenously powered by the export sector, the effect of the expansion of which worked through to industry and services. This took place within a polarized dual structure, where the bulk of production occurs in the modern sector but only involves a minority of the workforce, and where the ownership of the means of production was highly concentrated, forming the apex of the skewed income distribution. Nonetheless, the economy appears to have maintained an adequate rate of growth, destabilized only by excessive expansion of domestic demand, over the medium term, and it is clear that economic problems *as such* were not the cause of military intervention.

The contradictions are much deeper than this, and are all aspects of the duality of the system. In schematic form they are:

i) The highly concentrated ownership of the modern sector, and in particular the external dependence of the structure, results in the outflow of surplus, the alienation of decision-making power and the absence of either domestic technology or capital goods industry;

ii) The lack of integrated and sustained industrialization, due principally to the outward orientation of the modern sector and the narrow domestic market, itself the result of the personal income distribution;

iii) The neglect of the traditional sector, leading to a shortage of food supplies[56] on the one hand, and worsening of internal migration on the other;

iv) The decline in capital formation – reducing the possibility of economic development to continued export-led growth based on natural resource exploitation rather than autonomous reproduction.

It is these problems that the military government has been attempting to resolve since 1968. As we shall see, in Chapter 3, a fair measure of success has been attained with (i), while (iv) is being tackled through the state sector. Problems (ii) and (iii) remain as specific tasks for the future, the realisation of which may require further changes in the political structure itself.

NOTES TO CHAPTER 2

1. Marret (1969), a former British ambassador to Peru, gives a very good general introduction to the country.
2. Lewis (1954), Fei & Ranis (1964).
3. As in Baran (1957) or Griffin (1971), as opposed to a 'marxian' definition in terms of labour power.
4. On average, for the 1960–72 period, government expenditure was 16% of GDP, while gross capital formation was 19%: this sets the lower bound at 34%. Personal income distribution was such that the lower 75% of the population receives 25% of the income: defining this as the basic consumption requirement (a high value), then the upper bound is 67%.
5. Baran (1957) gives an excellent description of the paradigm. In the words of the military government:
   "Peruvian society is underdeveloped and dependent within the capitalist system". (INP, 1971).
6. See Appendix IV for a discussion of sources.
7. See Barraclough (1973) for an analysis of Peruvian agriculture in the context of a comparative study of Latinamerican agrarian structure, and Coutu & King (1969) for a description of output trends.
8. Barraclough (1973) gives the following geographical breakdown of land and families, based on the 1961 Census:

	% agricultural land	% families
Costa	7	6
Sierra	82	84
Selva	11	10

   but it should be remembered that the coastal arable land is mostly irrigated and the mountains mostly pastures.
9. The same source also gives the following land distribution in terms of unit size, a pattern repeated through the three ecological zones, but there is reason to believe (see Chapter 3.3) that the place of the 'middle farmer' is seriously underestimated.

	% of units	% of area
< 1 ha	34	1
1 < 5	48	15
5 < 500	17	19
500 <	1	71

10. Peruvian Times 'Mining Survey' (Lima, Nov.1974).
11. Roemer (1970)
12. ONEC (1973). For a fuller discussion of industrialisation during the 1965–75 period, see Fitzgerald (1975).
13. Beaulne (1974)
14. Saberbein (1973)
15. See Appendix I
16. CEMLA (1968)
17. Although the importance of rural traders should not be underestimated, as these include both locally powerful petty merchant capitalists and many of the peasant producers themselves.

18. See Appendix I.
19. A model of this process is proposed in Fitzgerald (1976). Simplifying this model, we can derive the essential result as follows. We define the modern wage (w), the modern labour force (L), the petty urban group (U) and the peasant labour force (A). We assume that the modern sector spends a certain proportion (b) on services, giving a determinate urban service income per head (bwL/U) which attracts migrants until it is depressed to the average rural income (a):

$$bwL/U = a$$

so that there will always be an urban 'pool' as a proportion of modern employment:

$$U = Lbw/a$$

and this determines the rural labour force as a remainder from the total (N):

$$A = N - L(1 + bw/a)$$

20. As they reflect not only labour productivity but also relative capitalisation and the factor price structure.
21. See Appendix I.
22. The top five products in 1973 (copper, fishmeal, zinc, sugar and coffee – in that order) differ markedly from the list for 1950 (cotton, sugar, oil, lead, copper).
23. Beaulne (1974)
24. INP (1974a)
25. Greater than 20,000 inhabitants.
26. This estimate is not very reliable, due to the difficulty of establishing employment in the traditional sector.
27. See BCR (1974a)
28. ECLA (1967)
29. BCR (1974a)
30. Income per 'agricultor independiente' deflated by GDP deflator and based on 1960.
31. The details of economic growth since 1968 are discussed in Chapter 5.
32. Thorp (1967)
33. See footnote 31
34. ECLA (1971)
35. Malpica (1967), (1974)
36. Espinoza (1971), (1972).
37. Espinoza (1971)
38. Roemer (1970)
39. Espinoza (1971)
40. Espinoza (1972), see also Thorp (1975).
41. Goodsell (1974), Ingram (1974), as well as the previously mentioned sources.
42. BCR (1974) shows the average ratio of exported profits to declared post-tax profits of all companies to be 38% for the 1960–68 period.
43. See Chapter 3.
44. The groups cited by both Malpica and Espinoza in their work are: Cerro, Grace, Copsa-Pacocha, Meise-Prado-Aguirre-Raffo, Ferreyros-Rizo-Beltran, Lercari-Aspillaga-Lanata-Bentin-Mujica. These groups all include agriculture, banking, industry and real estate, while some of them cover mining or fishing as well.
45. The banks associated with these groups and with the principle foreign owned banks, accounted for 73% of commercial business in 1969.
46. See the work by Torres (1974).
47. Bertram (1974) has an interesting discussion of this topic in the context of mineral exploitation in the first half of the century.
48. Of Kalecki (1972a) on the general context of financing capital formation in a developing economy, and Griffin (1971) in the specific context of the foreign and domestic savings in Latin America. Kalecki argues in terms of a demand constraint on total investment opportunities and thus alternative sources of financing become substitutes, while Griffin gives a cross-sectional analysis of domestic and foreign savings to demonstrate their substitutability in practice. This argument seems even in a priori terms to be more plausible than the 'two gap model' implications of finance being the

constraint on investment – beyond the tautological identity between savings and investment *ex-post*. This is particularly true in economies with relatively high average income per head and a concentrated income distribution and thus a large extracted surplus.

49. A topic considered in some depth in Chapter 4.3
50. The study of the flow of funds in the financial sector for the 1965–70 period contained in CNSEV (1973) illustrates this point. Of all the financial assets in private hands in 1970, 77% were held by financial institutions and the other 23% by households. Of the institutional holdings, 78% were held by commercial banks, the rest by 'mutuales' (10%), insurance companies (6%), 'financieras' (3%) and savings cooperatives (3%). Of the household assets, 43% are in 'mutuales', 25% in insurance, and 17% in savings cooperatives.
51. It should be pointed out that in the national accounts estimates of investment (and it is from this that savings are calculated) are based on sales of capital goods and thus not highly reliable, nor are they differentiated by sector.
52. That is, the loans for the private sector to the public less the loans from the latter to the former.
53. Based on fragmentary data for housing output, capital stock in manufacturing, and sales of transport equipment – all shown in ONEC (1973, 1971).
54. INP (1973a), which is based on the methodology applied by Harberger (1969) to the Colombian case.
55. As distinct from 'inequity' or 'injustice', a 'contradiction' must involve an inconsistency in the *functioning* of the system, eventually leading to stagnation or breakdown.
56. MinAg (1974).

3

Reforming the Pattern of Ownership

3.1 The Objectives of the Reforms

In this chapter we shall examine the reforms in the ownership of the means of production that have been carried out since October 1968. The extreme concentration of ownership[1] of modern sector assets in the hands of the domestic elite and foreign enterprise, was in 1968 most evident in land, export industry and finance, and it is these that have been the prime targets of a radical series of reforms in the 1969–73 period. The main result of these reforms has been to break much of the economic power of the domestic elite, to reduce substantially the foothold of foreign enterprise in the economy, and to introduce a certain degree of worker participation. This, in turn, combined with the expansion of public enterprise, has led to the emergence of the state as the dominant force in the economy. The process of surplus mobilisation has been fundamentally altered, but not so as to bestow total control to the state – as final domestic output remains in the non-state sector.

It is difficult to assess the extent to which the reforms have been part of an overall programme, but it would appear that some at least were the result of circumstances – particularly the need to execute wider policy in the face of current events. It is clear that, given the background to the 1968 revolution,[2] the large farms (particularly the coastal sugar estates), a number of foreign enterprises (particularly IPC and Cerro de Pasco) and possibly the major banks were originally marked for expropriation. Other reforms, however, appear to have arisen from policy implementation (such as the collapse of fishing) or the entrepreneurial inactivity of domestic capital. The introduction of worker participation, although it became a policy objective at a very early stage, took some time to develop as a coherent strategy, but what is clear, is that the 'key' reforms do reflect the realization by the military of a long tradition[3] of popular pressure against 'oligarchy' and 'imperialism'. It has also become plain, however, that these were far from being the only problems suffered by the Peruvian political economy.

The scope of the reforms extends to most of the modern sector, but as this only accounts for a third of the Peruvian workforce (distributed through all sectors) and represents a change more in ownership than in the 'vertical' relationships of production, it has not as yet contributed greatly to the fundamental problem of duality or the rationalization of production. In the long run, of course, the new role for the state and the new forms of ownership will have considerable significance, but the apparent lack of immediate benefits to the poor has led to some strain in the political system.

The different reforms are discussed in this chapter in four groups: foreign enterprise, agrarian reform, state enterprise and worker participation. These are followed by an attempt to establish, in quantitative terms, the scope of the reforms in relation to the economy as a whole.

3.2 The Exclusion of Foreign Enterprise

The treatment of foreign capital is central to the 'Peruvian model', and the activities of these multinational corporations were crucial to the political problems of the sixties. Here we are concerned with the changes in ownership and control, the general policy and bargaining issues being postponed until later[4], and we shall consider the former in two parts – firstly the specific expropriations, and secondly the general restrictions on the remaining foreign firms. In general, it would seem incontestable that the results of these reforms has been to reduce the historically excessive degree of external dependency suffered by Peru. This aspect of policy is that which, perhaps predictably, has received most international attention.[5]

Of the enterprise expropriations, the presence of two North American firms were specifically political issues in 1968 and thus the objects of special action. The first was the International Petroleum Corporation, which had dominated petroleum extraction and distribution, and this was immediately expropriated in November 1968, forming the basis of the state oil company (Petroperu), although the compensation negotiations remained a contentious issue until 1973. The second was the Cerro de Pasco Corporation, which dominated the mining sector and was also a substantial landowner. This was the subject of somewhat longer manoeuvring, but was finally taken over in 1973, becoming the public enterprise Centromin. In this way the government eliminated two historic 'bêtes noires', but could not enjoy the large profits that had been exported from them, because both firms required substantial recapitalisation. The reforms, moreover, did not affect the key mining company (Southern Peru Copper) and the other foreign oil company (Belco).

A large number of other foreign enterprises have been expropriated as part of general sectoral policy, although due to their predominance in these sectors, these policies were inevitably framed in relation to their presence. As a result of the land reform (see below) the Grace Corporation, accounting for half of all capital in sugar processing, was expropriated in 1969, production going to a cooperative and ancillary enterprises into the public sector. As part of the general reform of the telecommunications sector, both the I T & T and the (Swedish) telephone company were taken over, as were the foreign shareholders in the electric power companies, in 1969. When the fishing sector collapsed in 1973, and passed into state hands, a number of foreign companies (e.g. Starkist) were involved. As a consequence of the banking reforms in 1970, a number of foreign banks were nationalized in succeeding years – including Continental (Chase Manhatten), Internacional (also USA), Lima (French) and Credito (Italian) – as well as severe restrictions being placed upon the activities of the branches of foreign banks. In the transport sector, the British-owned railways have become state property, and perhaps more significantly, the US car companies (Ford, Chrysler and General Motors) have all left Peru after the vehicle assembly market was rationalized and one multinational (Toyota) chosen for a joint venture conferring monopoly control of the car and light truck market. Finally, foreign capital has been excluded from fishmeal (1969) and cotton (1974) marketing, equivalent to exclusion for a number of firms.

Despite these changes, foreign capital remains considerable in a number of sectors, particularly manufacturing and services. Although direct foreign investment has been effectively barred (apart from the key projects in oil, copper and chemicals) and there has been a considerable outflow of depreciation funds[6], the technological predominance of foreign capital (and weakness of Peruvian industry) is recognized by the government, and further cooperation with public enterprise is encouraged. The issue of technological dependency[7], however, is seen as important, and the 1970 Industries Law contains provisions both for the supervision of contracts and reduction of royalty rates, as well as checking on transfer pricing[8]. The Andean Pact provisions for the transference of majority foreign holdings to national ownership over the period to 1985 are being applied rigorously – and indeed Carlson (1974, p.8) concludes "it seems that only one country, Peru, is prepared to carry out the common rules on foriegn investment in a consistent manner". In consequence, the Andean Pact provisions for the limiting of exported profits to 14% on invested capital provide a real constraint. The reservation of certain production sectors to national capital, combined with the ownership and control changes mentioned above appear to have reduced the rate of profit outflow by two-thirds.[9]

The overall effect, then, has been one of considerable reduction of 'dependence', if this is interpreted in terms of foreign ownership, or of decisions made abroad, or of exported surplus, or of technological control. This represents, however, a 'catching up' with the errors of the past, and it may well be that the attempt to secure rapid industrialisation in future will cause some difficulties in the matter of transfer of technology.

3.3 Agrarian Reform

The major change in the non-state sector has been the Reforma Agraria, the agrarian population being over half the national total. The extreme maldistribution of land, and the capitalist exploitation of the large estates was the chief characteristic[10] of land tenure in 1968 – although the tenurial relationships exhibit considerable complexity particularly in the peasant 'communidades' and the multiple tenure of small plots in different ecological zones. The problem had been a major political issue in the past, and was one of the main items on the government agenda after the coup.

Under the Belaunde government[12], an attempt at land reform was passed into law, but there was no real effort at implementation, and the exclusion of 'agoindustria' (i.e. the sugar estates) and productive farms on the one hand, and the 'parcelación' (splitting up) of estates purchased by the government on the other were weak points. Very little progress was made under the 1964 law, and the effect was to exacerbate rural tension – apart from the guerilla activities there occurred a series of Sierra land invasions in the middle of the decade. In fact the traditional hacienda system was breaking down; the combination of weak agro-export prices and attractive urban investment opportunities, as well as the rural tension was already leading to the decapitalization of large-scale capitalist agriculture. It was against this background that the 1969 'Ley de Reforma Agraria' was established, with the declared objective of putting land "under the direct control of those who, with their labour, generate its wealth".

The application of the Law suffered modification[13], in the course of implementation but it is clear that the main initial consideration was the expropriation of the coastal sugar estates, with similar provisions for Sierra and Selva land[14]. It is this, with the low levels set on private holdings (150 ha on the coast, 30–35 ha in the Sierra and a similar amount in the Selva) which make it the most radical land reform in South America. Large estates have been turned over to the permanent workforce, creating a series of Cooperativas Agrarias de Produccion (CAP) on the coast and Sociedades Agricolas de Interes Social (SAIS) in the Sierra. Compensation is fixed by government tribunals, and mostly takes the form of government bonds, payable over 20 years at 5%, although they can theoretically be used as collateral for raising industrial investment finance.[15]

It was intended to affect some 10 million hectares (out of 24 mn) and benefit some 300,000 families in this process. In the event, by end-1974 some 4.8 mn ha had been affected to the benefit of 200,000 families, at a cost of 13 bn soles, and it is found that the process, working from the large estates downwards, is reaching the 'middle' farmers. This miscalculation appears to have been mostly the result of inadequate data[16], which underestimated the importance of medium farmers (i.e. large peasants) in agriculture. This particular land reform, therefore, is coming to a close with about 5 mn ha affected. The position is well represented by table 18, for a slightly earlier date, which shows the various recipients of land.

Table 18. Allocation of Land under the Agrarian Reform (to 30.3.74)

Entities	Number	Area (mn ha)	Families ('000)
CAP	287	1.35	79
SAIS	40	1.99	48
Comunidades	96	0.41	31
Grupos Campesinos	263	0.60	13
Other*	127	0.72	8
Total	813	5.07	179

Source: MinAg (1974).
*some 0.5 mn from pre-1968 reform

The main problem is that even though the major estates have been handed over to the permanent workforce collectively, this does not benefit the bulk of the agricultural workforce. This is for two reasons, firstly because the bulk of rural labour (about 60%) works on their own small plots, and so is not affected at all, and secondly because the seasonal labour on the estates (about 15%) cannot participate in the benefits of the cooperatives either – the profits going, logically, to the permanent members. Thus, the relative size of holdings has not been changed, nor has the structure and techniques of production – although it must be pointed out that the effective 'absorptive capacity' of the estates is not that large anyway. To a certain extent, moreover, it would seem that the reform beneficiaries have emerged as an elite within the rural sector, maintaining relationships with other peasants and wage labour remarkably similar to those of previous owners, and even retaining most of the managerial and technical staff. This has had the positive effect of maintaining production, but the government is well aware of the social implications, and apart from direct appeals to the 'cooperativistas' to treat wagelabour better, have started to establish Proyectos Integrales de Asentamineto Rural (PIAR). The PIAR's, which involve the inclusion of a large estate with the nearby communities and villages within an integrated project, are intended to distribute the bulk of the cooperative profits through the surrounding area. The majority of the peasants, however, have not benefited from the land reform precisely because they were not a direct part of capitalist agriculture.

Although the reform is 'agrarian', it is in fact mostly concerned with land tenure. The most significant supplementary legislation has been to do with water rights[17], an important means of effective control in irrigated zones when in private hands, which are now exclusively the property of the state. The main constraint on agricultural expansion, apart from the arable land area itself and long-term problems such as training and transport, appears to be the inadequate availability of inputs, and above all the means to purchase them. The bulk of state credit (and private bank finance) still goes to the large production units – although these are now collective enterprises rather than private firms[18]. Fertilizer production is being expanded, as it output of agricultural equipment, and irrigation projects are under way, but the weak position of the peasant farmer (and thus food production) still remains. Pricing policy, probably the best medium term means of encouraging production, is still geared to the maintenance of low urban supply prices[19].

In sum, then, the land reform has changed the pattern of ownership but not the structure of production or the allocation of labour to the land. The result is that only a quarter of the rural population has so far benefited from the land reform, this not being a policy decision but rather the result of the production system itself, even though raising the income of the peasant masses would depend more on productivity and prices than in tenurial relations. As far as the mobilization of the surplus is concerned, there are two important aspects. The first is that the transfer process implied by the internal terms of trade for food against manufactures remains much as before the reform. The second involves the profits from the estates. Taxes are payed more or less as before, but profits are not transferred into other sectors but rather retained as labour income or invested in the mechanization of the cooperatives. As a result, although the economic power of the landlords has been removed, the state has not acquired their control over the agricultural surplus.[20]

3.4 State Ownership

The expansion of the public sector is one of the main features of the reform programme, but, as we have already seen, it is as much the product of sectoral reform as a planned strategy in itself. By this, we do not wish to imply that the process was accidental, it has had its own logic, but rather that the expansion was partly the result of action taken to achieve other targets (e.g. reducing external dependence) or the means of attaining certain policy objectives (e.g. rationalization of fishing). In other words, the expansion of state enterprise has been seen, during the reform period at least, as a means rather than an end in itself. This has led to the creation of what is still a somewhat disarticulated state sector, as we shall see in Chapter 4. Here we shall discuss the origins of the enterprises themselves.

We can consider[21] these enterprises in three groups; those taken over from foreign capital, those previously owned domestically, and those originally established as public enterprises. In the first group we find PETROPERU (the state oil company, formed from IPC and the small state company EFP), CENTROMIN (the former Cerro de Pasco mining complex in the central Sierra), HIERROPERU (former Marcona iron ore operations), ENTELPERU (the former I T & T and Swedish cable and telephone firms) and ENAFER (the railways) operating as key sectoral agencies. In addition, there are a number of former foreign enterprises where the state is majority shareholder but which are still subject to private law. These include the results of the bank expropriations (Continental, Internacional, Lima and Credito), the non-agricultural interests of the Grace Corporation, and the urban electricity distribution companies.

In the second group, we find mainly the results of the collapse of the fishing industry. This arises from a combination of excess capacity and overfishing in 1971 and ecological changes in 1973. In 1971, a state corporation, EPCHAP, was set up to market all fishmeal, and in 1973 the main consortia were taken over, the fleets and factories rationalized, and the whole reconstituted as PESCAPERU. Partly as a result of this sectoral collapse, the 'Prado empire'[22] went bankrupt, and a series of key enterprises passed into state hands – including a major bank (Popular), cement, paper, fertilizers and textiles. This provided the opportunity for total control of cement, paper and fertilizers.

In the third group, we find the original state steel enterprise founded in 1964 (now SIDERPERU, and monopoly supplier), the hydroelectric system (ELECTROPERU), the fertilizer corporation (SENAFER, dating from the guano boom at the beginning of the century), the flag carrier AEROPERU (created in 1972), and CPV, the state shipping line. The public 'bancos de fomento' (Industry, Agriculture, Mining, Mortgage and Housing) have also expanded operations considerably. In mining, we find the new enterprise MINEROPERU (responsible for all mineral exports and joint ventures in mining), and in marketing CECOOAP (sugar sales) and EPSA (domestic marketing of essential foodstuffs, monopsony of food imports and a chain of supermarkets). In banking, COFIDE is now the exclusive financial intermediary for market finance to public enterprises, and a holding company, INDUPERU has been established for all state share-ownership in industry and for joint industrial ventures with foreign capital.

By these means, the state has gained control over one third of output and one fifth of the workforce in the modern productive sector (i.e. excluding government itself)[23]. This confers a determinate control over intermediate, but not final production – with a double implication. Firstly that the state corporations respond to demand patterns generated primarily in the private sector, producing inputs or foreign exchange for eventual use outside the state sector. Secondly, that the enterprises owned by the state are not, at present at least, substantial generators of profits, in fact they all have substantial net resource requirements. The direct control over the financial system and foreign trade, combined with the rigorous planning mechanism do give the state considerable power over the whole modern sector, however. The government regards the ownership reforms as being the completion of a particular stage:

> "The position of the state as leader ('conductór') of the economic process, will be consolidated, particularly in the context of petroleum exploitation,

mining, fishing, basic industry, electricity, communications, transportation, domestic marketing of essential products, external trade and the financial system." (PRP (1974), author's translation).

Although the organization of the state is analysed in the next chapter, it is worth discussing here whether this expansion is equivalent to the establishment of 'state capitalism'. If this is merely taken to mean a large state sector, then the answer is clearly affirmative, but not very useful. If the definition implies a situation where the state becomes a shareholder in capitalist industry without changing the mode of production, then this is partly true of the Peruvian case, but part of the circumstances of creation – and will change in the future. Finally, the definition might be framed in terms of a 'corporate state' but it is clearly too early to establish if this is an accurate description, because the state enterprise sector has emerged not through an ideologically determinate strategy but rather as the result of implementing government policy in separate production sectors. In consequence, the state enterprise sector in 1975 is made up of a heterogeneous group of enterprises, pursuing somewhat divergeant goals, and the task of full articulation lies ahead.

3.5 Worker Participation

The introduction of worker participation in both the profits and control of corporate enterprise is seen by the government as a central aspect of long-term policy, introducing a new form of relationship between capital and labour.[24] This takes three main forms, the industrial community, the compensation community and social property. All three are, in principle, means of gradually establishing effective control by the modern labour force of corporate enterprise.

The first, and most important of these is the Comunidad Industrial (CI), installed under the 1970 Industrial Law. This involves all private industrial firms of more than five employees, which must now allocate 25% of pre-tax profits to the CI (made up of all employees of the firm); 10% in cash and 15% in the form of shares, while allowing for CI representation on the board of directors. Over time, if there is no other equity expansion, this should lead to the CI holding equally that of the private shareholders, whereupon the process stops. In fact, this period is bound to be a lengthy one[25], and delayed by further private investment, but it does allow employees access to decision making. Moreover, it is possible for the CI to apply to the state for funds to buy shares in their own company directly. There are, undoubtedly, many ways of circumventing this law[26] but this is not the main shortcoming of the system. This, as in the case of agrarian reform, springs from the duality of the industrial structure itself. By end-1974, virtually all the eligible 3,700 firms had established a CI, covering some 245,000 workers, but this accounts for only 38% of the industrial labour force, even though in output terms the bulk of industry is covered – 60% of value added and 80% of fixed capital[27]. So far, gains to labour have been relatively small, but in spite of the strong resistance of private capital to the concept, CI has considerable implications for the future.

The second form of worker communities are the 'comunidades de compensación' that operate in the mining, fishing and telecommunications sectors, and to a limited degree in state industries. In the former case, there is a system of profit sharing between firms in the sector so as to balance up the wagerates – but has little significance as yet. In the case of public enterprise, the state is exclusive owner, so government bonds are issued to the CI in place of shares, and two workers appointed to the board of directors.

The response of the government to these problems and the difficulties of stimulating non-state enterprise expansion has been to create a new form of enterprise called 'Propiedad Social' in 1974. Social Property is essentially a state producer co-operative, which is set up with government finance and technical assistance. The two key points are that on the one hand, the government guarantees the market by imposing import embargoes and placing exclusive supply contracts, and on the other the rate of labour compensation is set by the state and the surplus returned to a central fund for the establishment of new firms. This is to become the priority sector in light manufacturing, supported by heavy industry in the public sector, and the basis of expansion of modern sector employment. Although, again, in the long run this form of enterprise may become dominant, the presently possible rate of progress is not comensurate with the underemployment problem.[28] Social Property does, however, form the prototype of a 'Yugoslav' type of worker management in medium-scale production, and the policy is to give preference to it:

> "Action geared to promoting the establishment and development of social property enterprises will be implemented, giving them:
> - technical assistance and credit
> - investment projects within the Andean Pact sectoral programmes
> - linkages with state enterprises in other sectors"
>
> (PRP (1974), author's translation)

3.6 The Resulting Ownership Structure

It should be clear from the preceding sections that there has occurred in Peru a radical change in the pattern of ownership of the means of production. Two themes emerge throughout the sectoral reforms – the replacement of much of the (unfulfilled) role of domestic capital by the state on the one hand, and the limitation of the reforms to the modern sector, and thus to the minority of the population, on the other.[29] The first appears to emerge naturally from the events since 1968, and is clearly related to the historical incapacity of the domestic elite in achieving autonomous economic development – which is the logic behind the military intervention. The second is a source of considerable concern to the government, but apparently impossible to resolve except by adsorbing labour into the modern sector. Control over the modern sector and the new state powers does mean, however, that the state has emerged as the 'national entrepreneur'.[30]

The theme of this study is the way in which the surplus is acquired and allocated by the economy, and in particular the way in which the state intervenes in this process. The reforms have affected the allocation of the surplus within the modern sector only, as the relations between this and the traditional sector remains more or less unchanged. Within the modern sector, the rate of surplus extraction would appear to be similar, the change being in the allocation between the participant groups.[31] Specifically, the share to foreign capital has clearly fallen, and also that of domestic capital, while that of the state and labour has risen. It would appear that these reforms have resulted in a redistribution if income downwards through the modern sector, particularly in the case of the agrarian reform and to a lesser extent to the of the Industrial Community, although Webb (1973) argues that the effect has not been very great.

It would probably be useful to attempt to quantify the effect of these reforms, but the lack of an adequate statistical base makes this extremely difficult. What we have done here is to estimate the distribution of output (value added) and labour (the workforce) between four main groups – the state, domestic capital, foreign capital and various forms of cooperatives.[32] As changes in the economy as a whole were also occurring during the reform years (1969–73), the figures have been standardised on the basis of the 1972 production structure.[33] On this basis, the 'pre-reform' (i.e. 1968) and 'post-reform' (i.e. 1974) ownership patterns were superimposed. The results are necessarily very approximate, but are of some considerable interest, as table 19 shows.

Table 19. The Pattern of Enterprise Ownership

	Pre-Reform		Post-Reform	
% of GNP	Output	Workforce	Output	Workforce
State	11	7	26	13
Domestic capital	30	19	21	11
Foreign capital	20	10	8	3
Coops. etc.	–	–	6	9
Total	61	36	61	36
% of Total				
State	18	19	42	36
Domestic capital	48	53	35	31
Foreign capital	34	28	13	8
Coops. etc.	–	–	10	25

Source: Appendix II

NOTES TO CHAPTER 3

1. See Chapter 2.5
2. See Chapter 1.3, and also Zimmerman (1974)
3. Mariategui (1927) contains the original and best statement of the radical view of Peruvian contradictions, while Haya de la Torre (1961) covers the APRA viewpoint in the 1930's.
4. See Chapter 5.3
5. See, for example, Hunt (1974), Ingram (1974) and Goodsell (1974).
6. See Chapter 5.3
7. See Espinosa (1971)
8. Carlson (1974) states that royalty rates in overseas contracts have been effectively reduced from an agerage of 8% in sales in 1970 to 2% by 1973. Transfer pricing,

particularly by overinvoicing on imported machinery, was a favourite means of capital export in Peru, and this means that the private investment estimates (particularly for 1965–68) are overestimated in the national accounts.

9. See Chapter 5.3
10. See Chapter 2.5
11. See Chapter 1.3 above
12. See Barraclough (1973) and Petras & LaPort (1971), the first part of the latter book contains an excellent analysis of the progress under Belaunde.
13. Harding (1974) points out that the original law provided for the splitting up of large estates (with the implication of creating a 'kulak' class) but pressure from coastal estate workers forced the abandonment of this aspect and recourse to the power of establishment of cooperatives. It is in this sense that the land reform can be said to have 'moved to the left'.
14. Although without, apparently, great thought about the different social structures in the three areas.
15. This has caused some comment, such as Quijano (1972) to the effect that the land reform was basically in the interest of the domestic bourgeoisie – which position has become increasingly difficult to hold in the light of subsequent events, particularly since very few of the bonds have been used as collateral in this way.
16. Smith (1975) has an interesting discussion of the problem. It would appear that the 1961 Census, used in planning the reform, and analysed in Barraclough (1973), was based on very rough estimates made for a different purpose.
17. Ley General de Aguas (1969).
18. In 1968, large farms received 44% of the 3.5 bn soles credit issued by the Banco de Fomento Agropecuario – in 1973 the cooperatives got 62% of 5.5 bn.
19. This is discussed further in Chapter 7.
20. Except in the context of agroexports, which with an overvalued exchange rate, means an effective transfer of surplus to the state, but this was available to previous governments too.
21. There is a lack of published data on public enterprises, and much of this data was directly gathered, but see BCR (1974) and INP (1974). The rapid expansion and style of naming public enterprises has given rise to a *limeño* joke that has achieved the status of 'public sector proverb'. The story relates that after President Velasco has died and gone to heaven ('cielo'), the Archangel Gabriel rings up St. Peter to be greeted with the response "CIELOPERU speaking".
22. See Chapter 2.6 above
23. See 3.6 below
24. This idea has a traditional place in Roman Catholic 'corporate' thought and admits of more than one interpretation. It can be seen as an attempt to break up class solidarity (i.e. by-pass the trades unions) as Quijano (1972) argues, but it is also the aspect of industrial policy which has most alarmed foreign capital, as Carlson (1974) points out.
25. Assuming, say, a 25% pre-tax profit rate, the CI would get shares worth 3.75% of the equity, taking 27 years at this rate to gain shares equivalent to the original holding. This could be delayed if the owners put more money into the firm, which would comply with government policy also. On this, see Llarena (1972).
26. For example, by setting up sales agencies (not liable to the CI) within a group, where the profits can accrue by appropriate transfer pricing.
27. Figures supplied directly by the Sectoral Planning Office, Ministry of Industry and Tourism.
28. It appears that about one million soles is needed to create a social property job, given the requirements of technological efficiency. Even if a target of creating 100,000 jobs were set for five years, this would involve an annual investment equivalent to the entire state investment budget for 1974. See also Abusada (1973).
29. Webb (1973) underlines this very well, pointing out that the reforms are concerned with *intra*sectoral redistribution of income, while it is *inter*sectoral transfers that are required.

30. See Chapter 6
31. Their *use* of it (e.g. capital formation) will be discussed later on.
32. The full calculations are given in Appendix II.
33. That used in Chapter 2.2

4

The Economic Organisation of the State

4.1 The Administrative Background

The principle aim of this chapter is to explore the organization of the Peruvian state in relation to its economic function, with particular reference to the mobilization and allocation of the surplus through the public sector. This provides the background to the following chapters on economic policy and development planning, and should itself be read in the light of the preceding chapters on the structure of the economy and the post-1968 reforms.

Formally, the Peruvian state is established in its present form under the 1933 constitution[1], with a republican structure and 'unitary' (i.e. not federal) executive, and although the elected legislature and presidency are now replaced by the military command, this is forseen under that constitution. The President since 1968 has been[2] General Juan Velasco Alvarado, representing the military as a whole, within which the normal promotion and seniority system is maintained. All key positions at the top level (e.g. ministers, heads of public enterprises) are held by the military, there being no formal civilian participation in government either in the form of political parties or individual figures[3]. However, the inclusion of so many professionals in the rapidly expanding state sector and the informal personal contacts of members of the administration ensures a reasonably effective 'feedback system' with the private sector. At present, the style of decision-making is very much along military lines and civilian advisers are consulted as to means rather than ends. It would appear, moreover, that 'ideology' is not a generator of strategy in its own right, but is seen as a way of 'cementing together' a set of policy objectives that have themselves emerged from a particular view of the Peruvian development problem.[4] This point is well illustrated by the following quotation on the role of the state from the 'Plan del Peru'[5]:

> "The overcoming ('superación') of the dependent capitalist model and underdevelopment requires the State to undertake a role of active participation as promotor and leader of national development, through its direct and indirect intervention in economic, socio-cultural and political activity. . . . A philosophy is proposed which attributes to the state the full capacity for directing action (acción directriz), as the total expression and pre-representative of society, and which corresponds to the power that the nation requires in order to promote change and redistribute resources and social roles which were the product of the predominance previously exercised by the dominant class."

The highest policy-making body is the Consejo Asesor de la Presidencia (COAP, the Presidential Advisory Council), made up of military chiefs and ministers, while the Consejo de Ministros (Council of Ministers, or cabinet) is mainly concerned with administrative decisions. Within the executive branch of the state, the various agencies (known as the Sub-Sector Público Independiente, SSPI) are directly responsible to the relevant ministry, and these latter are organized into four main groups. We can distinguish between 'general' (Presidency, Justice, Foreign Relations, Planning etc.[6]), 'security' (Interior and Defence), 'economic' (Finance, Agriculture, Food, Fishing, Industry & Tourism, Commerce, Energy & Mines, and Transport & Communication) and 'social' (Health, Education, Labour and Housing) portfolios. The relative importance of these groups is indicated in the expenditure distribution below. As can be seen from table 20, as far as current expenditure is concerned (approximately equivalent to manpower), security is predominant, followed by social services (much of this is education), but in terms of total expenditure and thus, perhaps, weight within the administration the economic ministries are predominant – due to their investment budgets.

Table 20. Public Expenditure by Function (1973)

Group	Current[a]		Capital[b]		Total	
	Soles bill.	Per Cent	Soles bill.	Per Cent	Soles bill.	Per Cent
General	4.9	10	1.9	3	6.9	6
Security	20.1	41	2.9	4	23.0	19
Economic	5.7	12	64.0	89	69.7	58
Social	18.2	37	3.1	4	21.3	17
Total	49.0	100	71.9	100	120.9	100

Source: INP (1974b).
(a) general government only
(b) entire public sector.

In spatial terms, the administration is highly concentrated on Lima: there is little or no regional devolution of decisions and the local power of the state is represented by the garrison commander and the prefect, this latter being appointed by the Minister of the Interior. There exist plans to 'regionalize' the administrative process, mainly by decentralizing the executive and then giving it control over that part of the budget spent on activities in that region. The problem with this is that most of the significant 'local' decisions have consequences at the level of the economy as a whole, and thus must be planned centrally[7].

It is difficult to comment objectively on the *quality*, as opposed to the quantity, of the public administration, but it would appear that the former has improved substantially since 1968 – both in terms of professional expertise and of dedication to the task in hand. A series of administrative reforms have been implemented, involving the rapid promotion of a number of younger technocrats (especially in the 'economic' ministries and agencies, which are those that have expanded most rapidly) with a desire to 'get things done'. It is a matter for some concern, however, that since 1974, when the pace of expansion and reform began to slow down, a certain degree of disillusionment has set in.

The 'style' of state intervention is well illustrated by the following extracts from the 1974 decree nationalizing cotton marketing:

> "Considering: That it is the duty of the State to channel the resources of the country to the benefit of the national economy, taking into account the interests of the majority;
>
> : That cotton is held to be basic to the economy of the nation;
>
> : That it is necessary to dictate measures which permit a rationalization of the present methods of commercialising cotton seed and fibre, in order to guarantee the producers a just return, secure an adequate supply for the national textile industry and to obtain the best prices on international markets.
>
> . . .
>
> Article 1: The State assumes exclusively the internal and external commercialisation of cotton seed and fibre . . . "[8].

In quantitative terms the most rapid growth in the size of the state since 1968 has been in the public enterprises rather than general government, current administrative expenditure having kept step with growth in the economy. Historically, the most rapid relative growth in the size of the state was experienced under the Belaunde Government (1963–1968), and in fact the 1968–69 deflation involved a reduction in public sector activity. The main change, however, is in the changing role of the state rather than its absolute size. Indeed, the previous table showed a level of current expenditure (14% of GDP in 1973) that is below the Latinamerican average and a share of capital formation that is not outstandingly high[9]. The comparison, however, is clarified if it is realized that the share of 'economic' ministries in Peruvian public investment is, by that standard, high, with a correspondingly lower share for education and health.[10]

In relation to the domestic economy, we have already seen (Chapter 3.6) how the state has expanded into areas of basic control in the primary, secondary and tertiary sectors so that in 1975, in round figures, the public sector handles nine-tenths of exports and half of all imports on the one hand and is responsible for about two-fifths of employment and one-third of output in the modern sector on the other. These figures possibly give a better idea of the scope of state activity than the previous table, and underly the process of surplus mobilisation and accumulation through the state.

This chapter is concerned with the economic aspects of the role of the state in Peru. In consequence, we shall not deal with a number of aspects of the functioning of the public sector – in particular the military and security services[11] on the one hand, the the organization of public education, health and housing on the other. We shall look, however, at the 'economic' ministries and agencies in some detail. First, we shall examine the general government accounts, which form the basis of public finance as a whole, giving particular attention to saving on current account and the combination of this with other sources of finance to provide for capital expenditure. Second, we shall analyse the economic function of the state enterprises, concentrating again on their part in the generation and accumulation of the surplus, as well as their role in changing the structure of production. Third, we shall look at the

Table 21. Measures of the 'Size of the State': 1960–75

	1960	1967	1970	1973	1975[a]
Value-added (soles bn 1970 prices)					
General Government	10.4	19.3	19.1	23.8	26.2
Other Public Sector	*1.0*	*3.8*	*8.3*	*12.8*	*31.4*
Total Public Sector	11.4	23.1	27.4	36.6	57.6
Share of GDP	8%	11%	11%	13%	22%
Fixed Investment (soles bn 1970 prices)					
General Government	1.3	4.8	6.4	8.9	–
Other Public Sector	*1.0*	*4.6*	*4.5*	*8.7*	–
Total Public Sector	2.3	9.2	10.9	17.6	28.5
Share of Total GFCF	16%	36%	36%	42%	51%
Propn. of GDP	3%	5%	5%	6%	9%
Employment (thousands)					
General Government	168	251	289	335	..
Other Public Sector	*11*	*19*	..	*66*	..
Total Public Sector	179	270	..	401	..
Share of Workforce	6%	7%	..	9%	11%[b]
G.Govt.Staff/Total[c]	26%	28%	27%	27%	..

Source: Author's estimates from various sources, principally BCR, INP.
(a) planned, (b) Chapter 3.6, (c) government 'empleados' over total 'empleados' in workforce.

system of capital finance for the public sector, examining the way in which funds flow through the system and fit into the pattern of capital accumulation as a whole.

4.2 General Government Finance

Here we shall examine the structure of general government finance, looking at the way in which current income is raised from taxation and the balance remaining after current expenditure put towards capital finance. In broad terms, the current account has retained much the same characteristics since 1960, which in turn means a low rate of government saving and thus a strain on capital finance.

We start with the consolidated[12] government account[13] since 1960, in order to view the present system in its proper context, the main aggregates being shown in the table below. Over this period, the structure as a whole has remained remarkably stable on the current income side, with direct taxation accounting for around a third of revenue, the remainder being indirect taxes and a small proportion of revenue from services rendered to the public. Of direct taxation, about one half is personal (i.e. 'income') tax, and the other corporation tax, while indirect taxation is roughly one third import tariffs and the remainder consumption duties, mainly

Table 22. Consolidated Government Current Account: 1960–73 (%GDP)

	1960–64	1965–68	1969–73
Direct Taxation	4.5	4.2	5.9
Indirect Taxation	10.7	12.9	12.9
Current Income	15.4	17.1	18.8
Current Expenditure	13.9	17.7	17.9
Current Surplus	+1.5	−0.6	+0.9

Source: see Footnote 13.

on luxury items. The 'degree of progression' in the tax system is a topic of some debate[14], but it would appear that almost all the tax is extracted from the modern sector (where, after all, most of the income and consumption is), and within this the topmost income strata bear lower rates than the others (evasion and investment incentives) so that the bulk of personal taxation is borne by the 'upper middle class'. The pressure of direct taxation as a whole is low, personal tax being of the order of one-sixth of taxpayers' income[15] and corporation tax about one-fifth of declared corporate profits[16]. Since 1960, the main changes have been the relative rise in import duty income under the Belaunde administration, which fell back after 1968 with import restrictions, and the improvement of direct tax collection under this government.

On the expenditure side, the broad components of current costs have also remained similar over time[17], although there has been a steady increase in the proportion devoted to security, and a rapid expansion of social expenditure under Belaunde. It was this latter, particularly education (a response to populist pressure in Congress) that led to current expenditure rising up beyond the expanded tax income from 1966 to 1968 and thus to the current account deficit which contributed to the economic crisis of 1967. Expenditure was cut back sharply by 1969, and the surplus was maintained until 1972, but overall this 'government saving' is very small both as a proportion of GDP and of state income, as we have seen in Chapter 2.

Fixed capital formation[18] by the central government has shown a longrun tendency to increase over time, although the table below shows the most rapid expansion to have been under the previous government, there having been a cutback in 1969–70 and the major expansion only in 1973–74, as we shall see below. The major items in general government fixed investment[19] have been, and still are roads and irrigation, which between them make up about two-thirds of the total, the remainder being mostly public buildings. The very narrow margin of savings generated in the general government account does not contribute greatly even to the capital requirements of central government itself, creating a considerable borrowing requirement, which under the previous regime was partially used to finance current expenditure as well.

The financing of this 'economic deficit' is made up of domestic and foreign borrowing or monetary emission, but cannot be considered separately from the financing of the state as a whole, as the central government acts as a channel for

Table 23. Consolidated Government Investment Account
1960–73 (%GDP)

	1960–64	1965–68	1969–73
General Government Fixed Capital Formn.	1.6	2.5	2.7
Government Saving (current surplus)	1.5	–0.6	0.9
Economic Deficit (borrowing reqmnt.)	0.1	3.1	1.8

funds into the rest of the public sector, so we shall return to this topic in the last section of this chapter.

We can now turn to a more detailed consideration of general government current account, starting with the income side. As can be seen from the table below, there has been some change in the composition of current revenue, the proportion of direct tax in the total has risen from 37% in 1969 to 42% in 1973, while the total tax burden itself has remained more or less stable around 19% of GDP. Although comparisons are difficult, neither of these figures would appear at all high by Latin-american standards[20]. Within the direct tax total, the personal element has grown more rapidly than the corporate, due to the large exemptions given to private enterprise in the hope of stimulating investment on the one hand and the improvement of personal and social security 'enforcement' on the other. The former involved the reduction of the mean ratio of tax to declared corporate profit from 23% in 1967–68 and 25% in 1969–70 to 21% in 1971–73, without achieving the desired revival in private investment[21]. Indirect taxation has shown a slow gorwth in import tariff revenue because, despite the import surcharge, the embargoes on durable consumer goods and the shift towards food and capital goods imports[22] (both exempt) has reduced the dutiable base. The bulk of indirect tax is now made up of 'timbres' (stamps) on consumer durables and transactions, and has responded to the domestic consumption expansion since 1970[23] as well as to the simplified collection achieved by rationalising the rates and classifications.

In order to evaluate the tax system, it is necessary to establish the relevant objectives, and we can distinguish three types. First, there is the need to finance the state and particularly to provide a balance for capital formation. In this context, it would appear that insufficient effort has been made to increase the total rate of extraction of, and thus extend state control over the surplus. Second, a tax system can be used as a means of adjusting the price system and thus affecting the allocation of resources in the private sector. The main example of this in Peru is the tax rebates offered under the Industry Law of 1970 and the Mining Law of 1971, which have failed to stimulate the private investment[24], and tariff protection for domestic industry has been superseded by direct import controls. Third, the tax system might be seen as a means of redistributing income, but there has been no explicit move in this direction, and as Webb (1972) points out, the incidence of tax by income group has remained broadly the same as that obtaining before 1968.

The capacity for tax reform is an interesting analytical issue, to which we shall

Table 24. Current General Government Income: 1969–73 (soles bn)

	1969	1970	1971	1971	1973
Profit taxes[a]	7.5	10.5	8.7	9.8	12.6
Personal Tax: income	3.0	3.5	4.2	4.8	6.4
social sec.	4.0	4.8	5.1	6.5	8.5
Indirect Tax: imports	7.9	8.1	8.9	7.8	9.1
other	13.8	15.0	17.9	21.4	23.7
Payment for govt. serv.[b]	3.1	3.7	4.0	5.0	5.4
Total Current Revenue	39.3	45.5	48.8	55.3	65.7

Source: BCR (1974a)
(a) corporate and export tax, (b) e.g. refuse disposal, fines etc.

return later, as the ease of reduction in the current income of any particular group defines the freedom of action of the state and indicates the power of that group to limit it. This is not the only issue, as both the benefits expected from the state and the capacity to pay are relevant, but the apparent reluctance of this regime to raise tax rates[25] when the burden of both personal and consumption tax falls on the 'middle' and 'modern working' classes reflects the perceived basis of government support. In particular, the virtual exemption of state employees from personal tax is felt to be an unalienable right – and these now account for half the workforce in the modern sector. To the extent that the maintenance of the present 'model' depends on more taxation, this would clearly be in their interest – but there is no evidence of any collective recognition of this fact. Corporation tax does, however, seem to be an area where considerable resources might be obtained (an increase of the mean rate to 30% would transfer 2% of GDP to the state), given the lack of resistence to reform from private capital. Finally, the virtual absence of urban property taxation represents a potentially important source of revenue, but this would bear not only on the income of the petty bourgeois but also on the only investment of the bureaucrat or officer.

Turning to the current expenditure side, we shall confine ourselves to a few general remarks. First that, after the initial cutback in expenditure as part of the 1968 deflation, there was a steady rise in relation to GDP, from 17% in 1969 to 20% in 1973. However, this was due mostly to the expansion in public debt interest payments (about half of which correspond to foreign loans) while personnel and other purely administrative expenses rose from 10% to 11%, which is remarkable in the light of the scale of state expansion as a whole.

The composition of current expenditure is difficult to define exactly, due to changes in administrative responsibilities[26], but table 25 shows the main changes in relation to the pattern obtaining before this government. As can be seen, there has been an increase in expenditure on security (mostly the armed services themselves) and a decline in the share of 'economic' ministries. The reason for the former should be clear, and the latter is due to the shift of emphasis from agriculture and transport, which were ministerial responsibilities, towards minerals and industry, which devolve upon public enterprise. Social expenditure has remained a steady pro-

Table 25. Pattern of General Government Current Expenditure 1963–73

Function	1963	1968	1973
General	4%	4%	10%
Security	32%	34%	41%
Economic	26%	28%	12%
Social	38%	34%	37%

Source: Estimated from ONEC (1971), INP (1974b)

portion of the total, but in fact within this education rose from 21% of current expenditure in 1963 to 27% in 1968 and 31% in 1973, mainly at the expense of health. There is no indication that current public expenditure has become notably more 'redistributive' since 1968, and the three items of greatest potential (agricultural extension, education and health) in this context still mainly benefit the modern sector workforce.

The major part of fixed capital formation by the central government is made up of transport (roads), agriculture (irrigation) and housing, as table 26 shows. Sectoral investment allocation is analysed in Chapter 6, but here the switch in relative importance of transport and agriculture should be noted, and also the relatively small proportion devoted to housing. The increasing importance of the 'other' item is mainly multi-sectoral agencies such as SINAMOS.

Table 26. General Government Capital Formation: 1969–73 (bn soles)

Sector	1969	1970	1971	1972	1973
Transport	1.66	3.17	3.25	1.80	1.75
Agriculture	0.52	0.82	1.10	2.06	2.51
Housing	0.28	0.59	0.31	0.55	0.45
Other	1.45	1.85	3.44	4.60	4.14
Total	3.91	6.43	8.10	9.01	8.85

Source: BCR (1974b), INP (1974b)

We can now put the pieces together in order to explore the development of general government account in relation to the economy as a whole. As can be seen from table 27, the general trend has been for current expenditure to rise more rapidly (as a proportion of GDP) than current income, and thus drive the account into deficit, repeating one of the weaknesses of the Belaunde government's fiscal policy. This deficiency in government savings is all the more serious when the expansion in the rate of capital formation is taken into account, leading to a widening 'economic deficit' which requires private finance.

In sum, then, the system of general government finance retains the essential characteristics established before 1968, and corresponds therefore to the 'support'

Table 27. Consolidated Government Account: 1969–74 (%GDP)

	1969	1970	1971	1972	1973	1974
Current Income	18.8	18.9	18.5	18.8	18.9	19
Current Expenditure	16.7	17.0	18.0	18.2	19.7	20
Current Savings	2.1	1.9	0.5	0.6	−0.8	−1
Fixed Capital Formn.	1.9	2.7	3.1	3.1	2.5	−4
'Economic Deficit'	+0.2	−0.8	−2.6	−2.5	−3.3	−5

Source: BCR (1974a) and author's estimate (1974)

role for the state. The weak tax base only just provides for current expenditure and so provides little for capital formation. The fiscal system does not act so as to significantly affect resource allocation in the private sector, nor has it been used as a means of redistributing income within the economy – being mainly a means of financing common services for the modern sector. The structure of general government finance does not, therefore, correspond to the new role of the state as 'national entrepreneur'.

4.3 State Enterprises

The main burden of economic transformation and capital accumulation in the public sector is borne by the state enterprises, which are the chief vehicle for the economic strategy of this government, and so, as Hunt points out:

> "In the next decade the Peruvian economy will prosper or atrophy according to the effectiveness with which the new public enterprises are managed" (Hunt, 1974, p.51).

Although a number of state enterprises existed before 1968, the most important being steel, hydroelectric generation and development banking, their record was not good, either in achieving their objectives or in generating profits[27]. They appear to have acted more in response to political pressure on the government for subsidised inputs to the private sector rather than as agents for development.

There are now some forty-five 'empresas estatales', covering most sectors and of very diverse origins. We have already seen (Chapter 3.4) how the overall nature of state enterprise expansion fits in with the ownership reforms as a whole, particularly the exclusion of foreign capital in export and basic industrial sectors on the one hand and the inability of domestic capital to develop the economy on the other. In minerals, the main state enterprises are PETROPERU (oil), MINEROPERU (mineral sales and mining) and CENTROMIN (Cerro de Pasco), while in agriculture there is CECOCAP (sugar exports) and EPSA (food marketing) and in fishing PESCAPERU (all fishmeal industry) and EPSEP (fishing services) – forming the basis of state dominance in the export sector. Turning to industry, there are ELECTROPERU (electric supply), CORSANTA (hydropower), SIDERPERU (steel) and SENAFER (fertilizers) with INDUPERU acting as the state holding company for new ventures. Finally, in transport there are AEROPERU (flag carrier), CPV (shipping) and ENAFER (railways), while in communications there is ENTELPERU (telephones and cables) and EMADI in housing. Other, smaller enterprises cover activities as diverse as hotels, industrial alcohol, salt and coca as well as the normal public sector activities such as ports, airports and water supplies. In the financial sector, apart from the Banco de la Nación (a new foundation to deal with all government transactions with the public) the only new enterprise is the COFIDE (the state merchant bank), the other development banks (agriculture, industry, housing and mortgage) having been set up under the previous administration.

To these state enterprises should be added a number of companies which are owned by the government as majority (or sole) shareholder, but which still operate under private company law. In this group fall some agro-industrial plant, cement and paper mills and three banks. There are also a number of 'institutos', 'beneficiencias publicas' and other minor bodies in the non-governmental public sector, but as these are not important to the economy and account for less than two percent of public expenditure, we shall not consider them separately.

The scope of the state enterprise sector is considerable, and has secured for the state direct control over exports, infrastructure, heavy industry and finance. However, there is little direct public activity in production for the domestic market – particularly final manufacturing. In consequence, although the state has power over the bases of production and accumulation, and thus potentially over the surplus in the rest of the system, it cannot determine directly the pattern of output for domestic supply.

We have already seen how rapidly public enterprise as a whole has expanded, but the only comparable and consolidated data available in any detail is for 1973. Although this does not, therefore, include either PESCAPERU or CENTROMIN (two of the most important enterprises) as these were nationalised during that year, the aggregate data do illustrate a number of characteristics of some interest. The INP classifies the enterprises into four groups – producers of goods, producers of services, commercialization and development ('fomento') banks. The total expenditure of the sector in 1973 was equivalent to 25% of GDP, although must of the current costs were in fact goods for resale by the marketing enterprises, and of this total expenditure nearly 40% was on capital account. The outstanding feature of the account as a whole, however, is the paucity of the surplus of current income over current expenditure which means an inadequate contribution to capital finance, the balance being made up transfers from the Treasury and domestic borrowing, a topic taken up again in the next section of this chapter.

The figures shown in table 28 are dominated by a handful of enterprises out of the sector – four firms (PETROPERU, SIDERPERU, MINEROPERU and EPSA) accounting for 83% of sales by non-financial enterprises, while three (PETROPERU, MINEROPERU and ELECTROPERU) accounted for 77% of fixed investment. Similarly, of the seven financial enterprises, three (COFIDE, Banco Industrial and Banco Central Hipotecario) accounted for 84% of bank investment in that year. The fact that those enterprises[28] under the aegis of the Ministry of Energy and Mines generated 57% of sales, 74% of fixed investment and 51% of capital stock in the state sector not only indicates the dominance of this portfolio within the group of 'economic' ministries but also underlines the 'national entrepreneur' function of the state, which is also reflected in the importance of the Banco Industrial within the 'fomento' group of banks.

The total assets of the non-financial enterprises total some 65 billion soles in

Table 28. The Economic Activity of Public Enterprises (soles billion, 1973)

	Goods Producers	Service Producers	Commercial-isation	Total Non Financial	Financial Enterprise	Total State Ent.
Current Income	8.42	6.75	30.43	45.60	10.00	55.60
Current Expenditure	8.24	6.63	30.58	45.45	9.17	54.62
Current Account Surplus	0.18	0.12	−0.15	0.15	0.83	0.98
Capital Expenditure:						
Fixed	4.40	4.19	1.36	9.95	1.76	11.71
Financial	0.47	1.24	0.05	1.76	20.08	21.84
	4.87	5.43	1.41	11.71	21.84	33.55
Total Expenditure	13.11	12.06	31.99	57.16	31.01	88.17
Economic Deficit*	4.69	5.31	1.56	11.56	21.01	32.57

Source: INP (1974c)
*Total expenditure less current income.

1973, which is of the same order of magnitude as the assets in the manufacturing sector[29], but the return on these assets is extremely low,[30] and even the exclusion of the subsidy operations of EPSA would only raise the overall return from 0.4% to 1.4%. We do not have data in the same form for the financial enterprises, but in 1973 the ratio of their economic surplus to capital and reserves was 11%, and although this is much higher than the rest of the state sector, it was lower than the rate of inflation in that year. Moreover, in this context it should be realised that a 15% return on the net worth of all state enterprises would have yielded sufficient funds to cover a third of their own capital needs, a sum equivalent to over a half of corporation tax income in that year[31].

Table 29. Asset Structure of State Enterprises (1973, soles billion)

	Net Worth	Other Capital	Total	'Return'*
Goods Producers	11.41	9.52	20.93	1.6%
Service Producers	23.07	14.41	37.48	0.5%
Commercialisation	2.10	5.10	7.20	–7.1%
Total Nonfinancial	36.58	29.03	65.61	0.4%
Banks: Capital and Reserves			7.48	11.1%

Source: INP (1974c)
*'current account surplus' (from previous table) divided by 'net worth' or 'capital and reserves'.

It is worth considering three of the more important enterprises separately, as these illustrate some of the general points that we shall make later on. The activities of MINEROPERU, PETROPERU and EPSA not only reflect two key elements in government strategy (the oil and copper projects on the one hand and the attempt to secure an adequate and cheap food supply on the other) but also themselves are the main means of achieving them.

MINEROPERU was established in 1970, with the task of marketing all mineral exports from Peru, eventually also to refine all copper and develop the unexploited mineral deposits that reverted to the state in that year. In effect, this left only Marcona (iron) and Southern Peru Copper (Toquopala and Cuajone) as important enterprises in private foreign hands, and the creation in 1973 of CENTROMIN to take over Cerro de Pasco led to a third of all mineral production being in the state sector in 1974. Over the medium term, the state controls all copper marketing and refining through MINEROPERU, iron through the virtual monopoly of SIDER-PERU (once it is expanded) and most other metals through CENTROMIN.

In the long run (i.e. 1980) MINEROPERU will mine about two-thirds of Peruvian copper output directly. This enterprise, then, has a central task both in the processing and marketing of copper produced in the private sector and also developing its own vast deposits at Cerro Verde (67 million tons fine starting 1977), Santa Rosa (1172 million tons fine starting in 1979) and Michiquillay (568 million tons fine, starting in 1979). To date, the main activity has been the gaining of experience in international marketing (not an unalloyed success as in 1973 it was operating only on a 5% margin on sales) and the zinc and copper refineries are both foreign turnkey projects. The Cerro Verde/Santa Rosa project, however, is being developed by MINEROPERU itself with the deliberate intention of gaining both technology and operating experience while subcontracting as little as possible – preparing for its future role as the largest single copper producer in Peru by 1980 and possibly taking over the remaining foreign operations subsequently. In 1974, there were projects costing some $1,000 million under way and under design by this enterprise.

PETROPERU was established in 1969 on the basis of the former Empresa Petrolera Fiscal (a small public corporation) and the International Petroleum Corporation assets in Peru, giving control over most of the existing fields (producing two-thirds of domestic requirements), refineries and marketing network. PETROPERU is responsible for the 'gestion empresarial del estado' in exploration, exploitation, refining and petrochemicals. This enterprise has placed overseas contracts for the domestic deficit and has expanded the national distribution network, but by far the most important of its activities is the exploration for and extraction of oil from the Amazon region. Although estimates vary, the anticipated offtake of 200,000 barrels per day by 1980 and a total investment of the order of a thousand million dollars seem reasonable – and the technical problems are enormous, including exploration in jungle conditions, transport of the crude from the wellheads by fleets of tugs and barges, and pumping it over the Andes by pipeline to the Pacific. For reasons of speed, finance and technology (discussed in the next chapter) it was decided to subcontract two-thirds of the concession area to foreign oil firms in exchange for half their oil output. This has reduced the strain both on finance and expertise in PETROPERU to manageable limits while assuring the state of about two-thirds of production, and in fact this enterprise has maintained its exploration and investment schedules very well, while the ownership of the pipeline will grant effective control over the profits from private oil. PETROPERU is not yielding large profits at present, particularly since even in 1974 it was costing domestic ex-refinery crude at US$4/bbl and importing at US$10, due to the constraing on gasoline prices since 1969. Investment plans for exploration (as at 1974) totalled some $150mn which, with the $350 million pipeline and other projects added up to an investment programme of $650 million.

The Empresa Publica de Servicios Agropecuarios (EPSA) was established in 1970 in order to handle external trade in foodstuffs[32], to control internal markets of certain key foodstuffs (particularly wheat, rice, meat and milk) and to extend certain support services (e.g. seeds and semen) to farmers. Given the concentration of the Ministry of Agriculture itself on land reform and the requirements of the large export-cooperatives, EPSA has been the main instrument of government policy in domestic food supply, which is principally a matter of securing adequate deliveries to urban areas at politically tolerable prices. On the domestic front, it was hoped that EPSA could, by reducing wholesale and transport margins, both hold down prices to the consumer and raise these at the farmgate – but in the event the former was only attained by the massive import of subsidised supplies. The latter was not achieved, and food output has continued to stagnate[33], exacerbated by administrative problems within EPSA itself. Sales in 1973 were equivalent to roughly one-fifth of the urban food supply[34], and by the end of 1974 the increasing domestic food deficit, the mounting costs of subsidising imports[35], several temporary shortages due to maladministration, and financial irregularities led to the creation of a specific Ministry of Food. On EPSA's function as a whole, and this applies to the new portfolio as well, two comments can be made. First, the subsidising activity is not really suitable for an enterprise, as it is the result of government policy and appears to generate 'losses' which then impair the accountability of the enterprise itself. Second, and this is more serious, the lack of a sectoral policy of investment and credit for peasant food producers is to blame for the problems in domestic food supply, rather than the marketing system itself.

Table 30. Economic Results of Three State Enterprises (1973, soles billion)

	Current Income	Current Expend.	Current Ac.Surp.	Capital Expend.
MINEROPERU	17.72	17.54	0.18	1.14
PETROPERU	7.52	7.32	0.21	4.84
EPSA	11.82	12.19	−0.37	0.19
Total	37.06	37.05	0.02	6.17

Source: INP (1974c)

The state banking system is composed of three parts: first, the 'central banking' system, made up of the Banco Central de Reserva (fiduciary issue and exchange reserves) and the Banco de la Nación (all government transactions); second the development banks (COFIDE, Banco de Fomento Agropecuario, Banco Industrial del Peru, Banco Minero, Banco de Fomento de la Vivienda and Banco Central Hipotecaria); and third, the government-owned commercial banks, known as the 'banca associada' (Banco Popular, Banco Internacional and Banco Continental) which were taken over in 1970–73. The first group is important mainly to internal public sector finance (see next section), and need not concern us here. The last group of 'associated banks' had not been, by 1975, incorporated into the state system in any meaningful sense, and continued to act more or less as private banks except insofar as they follow the sectoral credit directives[36] more closely than these. It is the development banks that are the core of state finance, and within these (1973) the Banco Industrial accounted for 57% of investment, the two housing banks for another 22%. All the development banks, naturally, supply long-term finance, but with the exception of COFIDE, this is confined to loans rather than share capital although they provide a sum equivalent to nearly two-thirds of fixed investment in the private sector. These banks, although they do not operate on purely 'commercial' (i.e. profit-maximising) principles, do conform to the criteria of 'banking practice' which means that funds tend to go to creditworthy (i.e. large) clients who, it would appear are not so short of funds themselves, but welcome the provision of cheap capital and the implicit state support that this provides. As we have seen, the state banking system does not generate large surpluses, and can only provide for a third of its capital requirements. The Corporación Financiera de Desarollo (COFIDE) has a special role within the state banking system, although it is still relatively small, accounting for only 12% of lending in this sector. Firstly, it has the function of 'merchant banker' to the rest of the state enterprises, particularly in the negotiation of suppliers' credits on their imports of capital goods, and plays a part in the national project planning system[37]. Secondly, it provides equity finance to the private sector (about a quarter of its activity) by taking minority shareholdings in new ventures which are considered to be of development importance[38]. Finally, the COFIDE was charged in 1974 with the finance of the new Propiedad Social sector[39] and thus is central to the generation of new cooperative enterprises and their financial supervision. The COFIDE, however, sees itself as very much an enterprise, and concerned with 'efficiency' in a microeconomic or financial sense, rather than either social considerations (e.g. employment) or strategic objectives such as the reduction of external dependency.

In relation to total credit in the economy (excepting that issued by the central government), the state share has risen from one-third in 1966 to two-thirds in 1974, mainly due to the creation of the Banca Asociada, as the table 31 shows.

Table 31. Credit by Development and Commercial Banks: 1966–74 (soles billion)

	1966	1970	1974
Development Banks	8.7	15.5	37.5
Banca Asociada	–	7.3	15.1
Total State	8.7	22.8	52.6
Private Banks	15.7	15.9	30.8
Total Bank Credit	24.4	38.7	83.4
State Share	36%	59%	63%

Source: BCR (1974c)

An issue that is normally taken up in a discussion of public enterprise[40] is that of 'efficiency'. Although it is not always clear just what is meant by this concept in practice, we shall consider two possible aspects – on the one hand whether the particular activities involved are carried out at minimum resource costs, and on the other, the extent to which these activities contribute to the development objectives of the state. Clearly, if profitability in any one year is taken as a measure of efficiency, then the Peruvian state enterprises are 'inefficient' – but this would imply a competitive market in their outputs, a long-run measure of profitability[41] and the criterion of profit maximisation. In the case of the export enterprises, working on world markets and trying to earn the maximum of foreign exchange, this would become relevant once the major projects are on stream, but not at present. In the case of enterprises operating on the domestic market, profitability is more a matter of government price policy than economies in resource utilisation, and thus no microeconomic judgement can be made. On the whole, however, it would appear that the larger and more 'dynamic' export and heavy industrial enterprises are more efficient in the first aspect, but that some of the smaller and 'stable' ones leave much to be desired.

Sometimes, the discussion of public enterprise efficiency implies a comparison with the supposed merits of private enterprise, but this has little logical meaning in Peru, for a number of reasons. First that domestic capitalists have been unable or unwilling to undertake these tasks, and in any case have established oligopolistic conditions conducive to inefficiency. Second, although foreign capital might well have been able and willing to undertake these tasks, a fundamental policy objective is to minimise external dependency, so that again a comparison on this basis[42] is invalid. Third, the objective of public enterprise cannot be profit maximisation *as such*, but rather contribution to the economic objectives of the state (which may, of course, involve generating a surplus) so that commercial criteria are not relevant in any case. This is not to suggest, naturally, that the Peruvian state enterprises are paragons of virtue or that they should not be subject to efficiency criteria of some form, but rather that these should differ from those of private enterprise.

The more important aspect, however, is the problem of integrating public enterprise activities both between themselves and into the planning system[43]. The problem arises because the government sets these enterprises specific goals and, in a sense, agrees to underwrite the resources required. This can lead to conflicts between one enterprise and another[44], but more seriously to a disregard for the 'externalities' of their operations[45] and overall policy objectives. In particular, employment creation and import-substitution tend to be over-ridden by the desire to use capital-intensive methods (and foreign equipment) in order to attain these goals as rapidly as possible. Nominally, the 'parent' ministries should be able to prevent this, but in practice the larger enterprises can effectively report directly to the highest governmental level and successfully demand the priority of their production targets. At present, moreover, the system of financial control over enterprises is weakened by the long delays in auditing and the system of granting non-repayable current subsidies and capital transfers from the Treasury[46]. However, it might well be argued that not only is this the price to be paid for a dynamic public enterprise sector, but that this is a logical aspect of the 'Peruvian model'.

4.4. Mobilising Resources through the State

We can now turn to one of the central themes of this study: the way in which the surplus is mobilised and allocated through the state. Unfortunately, the statistical information for an integrated treatment is not available[47], but the overall nature of the phenomenon is indicated by observations throughout the analysis and at this point we shall look at the way in which the capital flows discussed in the previous two sections fit together and relate both to the finances of the state and to the process of accumulation in the economy as a whole.

Table 32 shows the magnitude of the flows in relation to the economy as a whole. As can be seen, the flow of resources 'through' the state has increased enormously in size, involving massive borrowing and lending operations. The points of most interest are the relatively low levels of saving on current account and net foreign borrowing[48], and in consequence capital expenditure has mostly been financed by domestic borrowing. However, this latter involves borrowing operations far in excess of requirements, as the state acts as a supplier of development finance

Table 32. Flow of State Capital Funds: 1969–73 (%GDP)

		1969	1970	1971	1972	1973	1974
Sources:	Own resources	2.1	2.0	0.6	0.7	–0.5	–1.5
	Domestic Finance	1.3	4.7	8.0	7.4	8.2	n.a.
	Foreign loans (net)	2.7	1.2	0.5	1.8	3.8	6.0
	Total Sources	6.1	7.9	9.1	9.9	11.5	n.a.
Uses:	Fixed Capital Form	4.2	4.5	4.9	5.0	6.2	9.2
	Domestic Lending	1.9	3.4	4.2	4.9	5.3	n.a.

Source: Appendix III

itself. By 1973, the state was borrowing about half of private savings and relending a third, and as a whole the flow of funds through the public sector had risen from the equivalent of 6% of GDP in 1969 to 9% in 1971 and 12% in 1973.

This process of borrowing from and lending to the private sector admits of three interpretations. First, it might be regarded as a means of generating savings from the surplus that would otherwise be consumed. Second, it might be seen as involve the state in the reallocation of investment funds from one sector to another without increasing the total savings rate in the economy. Third, it might be held to result in the state borrowing from and lending to the same groups, subsidising them through the interest rate differential. The first increases the rate of accumulation, the second leaves it unchanged but changes its direction, while the third might actually reduce it. Insufficient evidence is available at present to judge this issue, but the structure of savings as a whole would seem to indicate[50] that the first is not of great importance, and while there is some suspicion[51] that the third does occur, it is the second process that is the most important. The state acts as banker, supplying capital finance equivalent to nearly two-thirds of all private fixed investment[52]. Potentially, the control that this affords, combined with the operation of the 'banca asociada', should allow the state to determine the form of private investment, in relation to both sectoral allocation and choice of technique – even though these funds originally emenate from the private sector itself. However, this power has not yet been utilised by the state, as the development banks are not integrated into the planning system. Moreover, this control is largely a 'rationing' one, as it is difficult to persuade the private sector to undertake tasks that it is unwilling to consider in the first place. Nonetheless, if suitably deployed, this instrument could be an effective means of bringing the private sector into line with development objectives.

The main point to be borne in mind, however, is the totally insufficient 'own resource' base of state accumulation which could only be remedied by heavier tax pressure or larger public enterprise surpluses. This situation forms a contradiction in the new role of the state in Peru – although it is required to undertake the bulk of the investment programme it is not granted the bulk of mobilised surplus (i.e. saving) and thus must rely on domestic borrowing, although it does act as banker for over half of private capital funds.

Having examined the real resource flows in a national accounting framework, we can now look at the financial structure of public sector capital expenditure as presented in the government accounts and consolidated in INP (1974b) for 1973.[53] In that year General Government accounted for 45% of fixed capital formation, but bore most of the debt servicing, while state enterprise accounted for 53% of fixed capital formation but most of financial investment, through the state development banks. Two particular points of interest are the 'intrasystem transfers' of 5 billion soles from the Central Government to the State Enterprises, and the 'financial investment' of the former, which is mostly in fact the agrarian reform debt. The overall matrix illustrates clearly, moreover, the way in which the central government channels funds through to state enterprise fixed capital formation and lending to the private sector.

Table 33. Pattern of State Capital Expenditure
(soles billion, 1973)

	General Govt.	State Entpr.	Other P.Sec.	Total P.Sec.
Fixed Cap.Formn.	8.7	10.3	0.5	19.5
Financial Inv.	0.8	18.5	0.7	20.0
Cap.Transfers	6.2	0.6	–	6.8
Debt Service	21.4	4.2	–	25.6
Gross Total	37.1	33.6	1.2	71.9
Intrasystem Trans.				6.1
Net Total				65.9

Source: INP (1974b)

The financing of this capital expenditure can only be considered for the state as a whole, because although funds are destined for a particular agency and nominally assigned to a particular purpose (e.g. debt service) they in fact add to the capital resources of that agency in general. Again, we must confine ourselves to the 1973 figures, but these illustrate the system very well. The main source of funds is the Treasury (part of the Ministry of Finance) which provides capital for the General Government itself (and thus for most of the public debt servicing) and large transfers to state enterprise. The large items for 'own resources' in both General Government and State Enterprise are mostly amortisation funds and thus do not correspond to the 'national accounting' table explored previously. Finally, the general approach is for the central government to contract external debt and the state enterprises internal debt (i.e. bank borrowing), although COFIDE, PETROPERU and ELECTROPERU received external finance on their own account in 1973. It is also worth noting that most of the state enterprise bank borrowing (81% in 1973) is from the public Banco de la Nacion.

It is difficult to comment on the system in more detail without the information needed to disentangle the public sector public accounts. Nonetheless, there are some important points that bear mention. Firstly, *net* foreign finance has been a relatively unimportant source of finance for capital accumulation, and when combined with the lack of significant net surpluses on government current account and

Table 34. Pattern of State Capital Finance (soles billion, 1973)

	Central Govt.	State Entpr.	Other P.Sec.	Gross Total	Intrasyst. Transfers	Net Total
Treasury	24.0	–	–	24.0	6.1	18.0
Own Resources	1.4	11.6	1.0	14.0	–	14.0
Internal Debt	0.3	10.3	–	10.6	–	10.6
External Debt	11.0	6.7	–	17.7	–	17.7
Transfers	0.4	5.1	0.2	5.7	–	5.7
Total	37.1	33.6	1.2	71.9	6.1	65.9

Source: INP (1974b)

net public enterprise profits, the main sources of funds are naturally amortisation funds and domestic borrowing. The former represent, in essence, an accounting device in the case of the central government and the consequence of transferring capital 'free of charge' to the state enterprises, while the latter appears to effectively involve the state issuing credit to itself – with potentially serious inflationary consequences.[54]

As far as the future organization of these flows is concerned, current government reforms involve the establishment of COFIDE as the sole financing entity for state enterprises and the Ministry of Finance (i.e. the Treasury) the sole body for the central government and the rest of the public sector. The financing process remains, however, a means of 'catching up' with the activities of the public sector and 'balancing the books' with internal credit rather than a positive system of resource allocation. But on the investment side, the division of responsibility for physical (i.e. non-paying) infrastructure to central government and productive and financial investment to the state enterprises is an undoubted organisational improvement.

4.5 Problems in the Economic Function of the State

The economic role of the Peruvian state has expanded extremely rapidly since 1968, mainly through the acquisition of existing enterprises and the raising of the rate of capital formation. The administration of the government has been reformed, but retains the structural characteristics of the 'support' state of a typical Latinamerican economy, although the restraint in the expansion of general government is remarkable. The state enterprise sector has been extended rapidly into exports, heavy industry, marketing and development finance – but the main emphasis is on mining and oil. The main enterprises have met with considerable success in the attainment of output objectives, but display a lack of integration to the development progress. As far as the expansion of modern sector production, the raising of the rate of accumulation and negotiating with foreign capital are concerned, the Peruvian state has met with considerable success, although on distributive objectives the record has not been so good.

However, it was forseen that the state would not only be the national entrepreneur but also provide a large amount of its own resources for capital formation. As the 1971–75 Plan pointed out:

"The responsibility assumed by the Public Sector requires that it continues to strengthen its financing capacity, establishing a solid structure of resource acquisition which in part will be obtained through tax reform, appropriate programming of the internal debt and recur to external debt only in a rational form – so as not to aggravate the problems of external debt service. Also, great emphasis will be given to a greater acquisition of resources by the entrepreneurial activity of the State, and the increased efficiency of the state enterprises so that these can generate profits to contribute to their own finance." (INP (1971a), p.31, author's translation)

This objective has not been achieved, for three reasons: first, the inheritance of the old fiscal system, second the low return on the public corporations and third the fact that the main state enterprises are in the process of capitalisation. In consequence, as we shall see in the next chapter, the external debt has risen to a dangerous level. Similar proposals for reform are expressed in the 1975–78 Plan[55], but even if the financial problem were resolved by higher taxes or public enterprise profits (as they will be eventually with the mineral projects), the lack of control over production for the domestic market on the one hand, and the limited scale of social expenditure on the other do mean that the achievement of 'development' as opposed to 'growth' is not as great as it might be.

NOTES TO CHAPTER 4

1. Pike (1967)
2. To August 1975, at least, the 'succession' already having been established in the form of General Morales Bermudez, formerly Chief of Staff.
3. The centre and right parties appear to have faded away since 1968, although none have been proscribed – the only active ones remaining are the CP and the APRA. The national daily press and braodcasting has been directly controlled by the state since 1974, but this has not really represented a great loss, as it was controlled by the oligarchy before 1968 and effectively censored after that. Reasonable freedom of speech and publication appear to be maintained, however.
4. Although it is possible to find the 'origin' of particular concepts in the 'thought' of APRA or the Christian Democrats, this is to miss the point.
5. INP (1971a) pp.76, 77. Author's translation.
6. Among the 'etcetera' we find the Sistema Nacional de Movilisación Social (SINAMOS, National System of Social Mobilisation), the function of which is to mobilize support for the government among the masses, and for which purpose it controls considerable funds for the provision of small-scale public works, but to little avail – for which reason it has declined in importance since 1973.
7. Such as mining projects, for example. See Chapter 6.
8. Decree-Law 20736 of 17.9.74, author's translation.
9. Fitzgerald (1974) gives the following figures for 1970:

Country	Current Govt. Expand./GDP	State GFCF/ Total GFCF
Argentina	17%	41%
Brazil	24%	52%
Chile	26%	56%
Colombia	11%	34%
Mexico	15%	35%
All Lat.Amer.	18%	36%

10. Fitzgerald (op.cit.) gives a mean share for these five economies of 66% in 1970, as opposed to 89% for Peru in 1973, moreover the proportion of infrastructure within this is low by Latinamerican standards.
11. It is worth making two points in this context, which although not directly connected to this study are certainly relevant. The first is that the traditional military threat from Chile has attained a new reality since 1973. The second is that the degree of internal violence is, by Latinamerican standards, very low – the 1968 coup itself being bloodless and involving very few exiles.
12. Includes the local government as well as strictly 'central' government but the former accounts for less than 5% of income and expenditure, and is not worth considering separately.
13. The source for government accounts is essentially the Cuenta General de la Republica, but the classification and adjustment of these accounts employed by the Central Reserve Bank is relied upon here – see Appendix IV.
14. Hunt (1971), Webb (1972), both of whom argue not only that the tax system was already progressive, but that it has become slightly *less* so.
15. Webb (1972)
16. From BCR (1974a)
17. There is considerable difficulty in exact analysis of sectoral allocation of current expenditure over time, due to the changing number and coverage of various portfolios, so that any allocation is only approximate.
18. We shall consider total capital expenditure, which includes transfers to the rest of the public sector and debt repayments, in the last section of this chapter. Here we are concerned only with the 'economic' or 'national income' flows.
19. See Chapter 6.4
20. The comparative figures for the five largest Latinamerican economies are given in Fitzgerald (1974a) for 1970:

	Tax/GDP	Direct/Total
Argentina	15%	36%
Brazil	27%	29%
Chile	22%	43%
Colombia	13%	44%
Mexico	10%	53%

21. See Chapter 5.2
22. Idem
23. Idem
24. Idem
25. Budget speech by the Minister of Finance, 'El Peruano' (Lima, 2.4.75).

26. For example, the 'grassroots' projects formerly carried out by the now-defunct Ministry of Development (economic) are now the responsibility of SINAMOS (general) – approximate correction for this sort of thing would raise the 1973 'economic' figure to 17% and reduce the 'general' to 5%.
27. CDES (1965).
28. Principally PETROPERU, MINEROPERU, ELECTROPERU and CENTROMIN.
29. Reported by the Ministry of Industry to be of the order of 50 bn in 1973.
30. This would be even lower if the assets were revalued at replacement cost so as to take inflation into account. See Fitzgerald (1974a) on this point in general.
31. That is, some 7 billion soles as opposed to 13 billion in profit tax in 1973.
32. Except for sugar, handled by CECOCAP
33. See Chapter 5.4
34. EPSA sales of 12 billion soles in 1973 should be compared with the gross value of food supply to urban areas, about one third of one half of GDP, or 60 billion soles.
35. In 1973, almost all the losses of EPSA were in fact the result of importing wheat at $110 a ton and selling it at $70.
36. See Chapter 5.4
37. See Chapter 6.3
38. Such as the Bayer pharmaceutical project and Amazon sawmills, although some of COFIDE's other investment (e.g. Lima property companies) are questionable.
39. See Chapter 3.5
40. See, for example Hanson (1965).
41. Such as the internal rate of return over an extended period, including the future, presumably.
42. Such as 'is it cheaper in, say, balance of payments terms for PETROPERU to get the oil out of the Amazon itself or allow Occidental to do it?' It is similar to the attempt to reduce the dependency issue to the profitability of foreign investment.
43. On this latter see Chapter 6.
44. A notorious case is the metal pollution of the river Mantaro by CENTROMIN which is damaging the hydroelectric turbines of ELECTROPERU downstream.
45. For example, the effect upon the Amazon region in general (and Iquitos in particular) of the oil exploration boom and its imminent rundown are not considered by PETROPERU to be its concern.
46. After all, the 'power of the purse' is the most effective form of control in the public as well as the private sector.
47. See Appendix III for a discussion of cources and methods.
48. Fitzgerald (1974) shows that for the other six leading Latinamerican economies in 1970, the mean public fixed investment rate of 7% of GDP was financed as follows: own resources 2%, foreign borrowing 1% and 'domestic finance' 4%.
49. It is extremely difficult to establish the true rates, as the commercial banks will take up Treasury stock in order to use it as reserves and expand their own lending operations at profit.
50. This topic is discussed in both Chapters 2 and 5.
51. The data is, naturally, confidential.
52. That is, 5.3% of GDP in 1973 divided by 8%.
53. Unfortunately this has not been done for previous years, but it would be a most worthwhile exercise, as the figures for any one year may be misleading.
54. The scale of this is hard to estimate: the amount issued in 1973 was equivalent to 3% of GDP but the net effect would depend upon the relative flexibility of public and private prices. It is not clear, moreover, whether this method of deficit financing *causes* the inflation or is itself merely the consequence of adjusting to it. For a good discussion of the former 'monetarist' with the latter 'structuralist' case in the Latinamerican context, see Thorp (1971).
55. PRP (1974).

5

Economic Policy since 1968

5.1 The Objectives of Economic Policy

In this chapter we shall examine the evolution of economic policy since 1968, with particular reference to the short-term management of the economy. Although the nature of the regime means that there has not been much public or published discussion of policy,[1] this chapter explores the logic of a current state intervention which is of interest not only in itself but also in illustrating the nature of the new political economy. Economic policy since 1968 has emerged within changing circumstances but has been guided by certain general principles, constrained within the structure of the economy itself. We shall examine first the conduct of domestic economic policy over the 1969–74 period, and second the process of negotiation with foreign capital over the same period, concluding with some general remarks on the management of a dual economy such as the Peruvian one.

The objectives of domestic economic policy are two. The first has been to maintain economic growth during the period of ownership reforms, securing monetary stability and balance of payments equilibrium. The second is the rationalisation of basic industry and rapid capital formation in the export sector. There have been considerable difficulties, however, in reviving private investment and securing an adequate urban food supply.

The objectives of external policy[2] with respect to foreign capital are straightforward – to negotiate the two key extractive projects (oil and copper) and adequate external finance for the public sector while carrying through the exporpriation of major US firms and restricting the activities of foreign enterprise as a whole. The mounting external debt, however, reflects both financing difficulties and the shift away from foreign direct investment towards state borrowing abroad.

As a whole, the objectives of economic policy have been achieved. Economic growth was maintained over the period despite the collapse of the fishing sector, and a start has been made on the rationalisation of basic industry, although agriculture and private investment remain weak. The two export projects are well under way and the key foreign enterprises in state hands, although the burden of the external debt has increased. The main remaining problems of economic policy are the low levels of domestic food output and the inadequacy of investment in final manufacturing, which reflect the contradictions of this degree of state intervention in a dual economy. Both problems logically require for their resolution a massive reduction in urban, modern-sector consumption to enable the surplus to be reallocated (probably through the state) to raising productivity in agriculture and manufacturing.

As we have already noted in the previous chapter, the centre of economic policy-making, as in other matters, is the COAP with the INP as secretariat. The main executive agency will, in these situations have considerable impact on policy as well and in this context it is interesting to note that this weight lay originally with the Central Reserve Bank, but during 1973 appears to have shifted to the Ministry of Finance. This shift represented a change from the 'orthodox monetarism' of the reform period to a more active intervention in the economy since 1973.

5.2 Steering the Domestic Economy

The objective of short run economic policy in the 1969–73 period was, in the words of the Central Bank:

> "The Government . . . orients its actions in order to achieve a solid financial situation which permits it to carry out the programmed changes in the economic and social structure"[3]

In other words, to 'hold the fort' during the reform period. This must be seen in the context of a long-run policy objective consisting in the rationalisation of production in the modern sector, which we have discussed in the last chapter, and will return to again, although our immediate concern is the conduct of short-run domestic economic policy.

We shall turn, therefore, to the progress of domestic production as a whole over the period under consideration[4]. The Belaunde deflationary policy after the devaluation of 1967 consisted in reductions of public expenditure, credit restrictions and import curbs, and this policy was maintained by the military government into 1969, further strengthened by the imposition of a 10% import surcharge, prohibitions on certain sumptuary and competitive imports, and the tightening of credit restrictions. Agriculture suffered from both drought and weak world prices, there were strikes in the mines, and fishing reached its biotechnical limits, making state intervention necessary in order to limit catches. Manufacturing grew only slowly, due to political uncertainty and lack of credit, and construction reacted to the cutbacks in public investment. 1970 saw a recovery in output growth as a whole, as fishmeal exports rose into higher world prices, while agriculture, mining and manufacturing revived. The uncertainty in the private sector continued, due to the land reform (although this did not affect agroexports unduly) but the excess capacity in industry allowed expansion in response to increased export income to take place without further investment. This recovery was not sustained into 1971, as export growth slowed down again due to mining strikes (pressure for nationalisation) and another bad fishing year. Internal demand was maintained by the government through the expansion of bank credit, sustaining manufacturing growth, particularly in foodstuffs, automobiles and household equipment.

By 1972, the massive expansion of public investment began to work through the economy, providing an alternative growth factor to exports, so that in spite of poor agricultural results (rain this time) and the ecological collapse of the fishing sector[5] a satisfactory rate of output growth overall was maintained. Manufacturing and construction accelerated under the effects of protected markets and income redistribution for the former and state contracts for the latter. The effect of the fishing collapse was felt into 1973, however, and the government's expansion of both investment and bank credit could sustain growth in construction but not in manufacturing, which had reached full capacity and begun to impose a severe strain on imports. Policy in 1974, therefore, was geared to the maintenance of export growth and the restriction of imports – which was mainly achieved by fishmeal sales out of stocks and direct quota restrictions on imports other than food and capital goods. Manufacturing, construction and agriculture maintained their growth, but there was increasing concern about urban food supplies, the concentration of manufacturing growth in consumer durables and rapidly rising prices.

Table 35. Sectoral Growth Rates (value added at 1963 prices)

	1969	1970	1971	1972	1973	1974	1975*
Agriculture	6.6	7.8	3.0	0.0	2.4	1.8	3.0
Fishing	–10.0	3.3	–13.6	–48.4	–22.6	51.8	30.2
Mining	9.9	5.1	–3.5	4.8	1.5	4.8	6.0
Manufacturing	2.1	10.2	12.1	12.7	7.5	8.0	8.0
Construction	6.7	13.6	10.5	12.4	8.2	12.0	14.0
Material Production	2.7	9.8	5.7	5.7	5.8	7.0	7.6
Non-Material "	5.8	4.5	4.5	6.0	6.2	6.3	5.9
Gross Domestic Product	4.1	7.3	5.2	5.8	6.0	6.7	6.8

Source BCR (1974a), INP
*Planned

Industrial production has grown rapidly overall, but within the total some interesting variations have emerged. The first is the initial rapid recovery of consumer goods (food, drink, tobacco, textiles, shoes) after the 1967–68 deflation, but as these branches expanded into excess capacity the rate of growth slackened slightly. Intermediate goods production has grown steadily, an interesting point being the acceleration in non-metallic minerals (mostly cement) in response to the expansion in public investment. However, the really rapid growth has been in the so-called 'capital goods' branches (metal products, machinery and transport equipment), but most of this phenomenon appears to have been the sudden expansion of output of 'linea blanca' items (i.e. household equipment) as a result of import embargoes and the effects of the ownership changes (particularly land reform) on consumer demand. Table 36 shows the main branches, which account for some five-sixths of value added in manufacturing.

Overall, then, the main features of economic growth during the period have been the slow growth of agriculture, the collapse of fishing, the rapid growth in manufacturing[6], the acceleration of construction and the swelling of the service sector. The relative neglect of food agriculture, which might well have been revived with credits and higher prices, was a policy decision (albeit by default) to concentrate on the reform of tenure relationships in the modern agroexport sector[7]. The fishing collapse was beyond government control, and the reaction in terms of nationalisation and rationalisation was the best policy choice under the circumstances. The manufacturing boom was also the consequence of policy on import restrictions and credit to industry, but the government failed to revive private investment in this

Table 36. Industrial Growth by Main Branch: 1968–73

Selected Branches	Growth Rate[a] (% p.a.)		'Weight'
	1968–70	1971–73	(1973)[b]
Food, drink, tobacco	11.4	8.9	0.27
Textiles, shoes etc.	20.6	11.1	0.15
Paper	10.0	10.4	0.03
Chemicals	17.3	14.1	0.13
Non-met. Minerals	3.3	17.6	0.05
Basic Metals	9.2	35.0	0.04
Metal Products	15.5	18.0	0.05
Non-elect. Mach.	16.7	21.0	0.04
Elect. Machinery	16.1	25.0	0.05
Transport Equip.	−3.7	17.5	0.04

Source: Min. Ind. (directly)
(a) in value-added at 1970 prices
(b) proportion of value added at 1970 prices

sector. Construction, of course, has mostly benefitted from state capital formation. The expansion in the service sector, however, was caused by the stagnation of food agriculture and the consequent migration to the towns rather than any real growth in output.

The visible trade account reflects these developments in the domestic economy. The main feature on the export side has been the slow expansion in mining production and weak copper prices in 1971 and 1972, and the collapse of the fishing sector, exacerbated by fixed-price contracts negotiated by the government onto a rising world market in 1972. Overall, however, the unit value of exports (i.e. sales divided by tonnage) has moved upwards over the period. On the import side, the growing dependence on food imports on the one hand, and the reduction in consumer imports on the other are to be noted – the latter being the consequence of the import controls discussed above[8]. The import price index reflects the changing composition as well as rising world prices, but its wide fluctuations are difficult to explain. In consequence, the interpretation of the 'terms of trade' (i.e. the ratio of the two price indices) is almost impossible, but there has clearly been a general improvement – in line with the position of primary producers in the world as a whole.

Two general points should also be made. First, there has been little success in stimulating manufactured exports (much of the recent growth in the 'other' items is cotton textiles) and although the Andean Pact provisions may provide markets for these[9], the export mix for the forseeable future will be dominated by processed primary products. Second, the structure of industry[10] (which accounts for two-thirds of imports) is such that the expansion of domestic economic activity tends to lead to accelerated imports and potential payments disequilibrium. Import controls such as those imposed by this government are an effective temporary measure, but clearly in the long run the solution lies in a more effective integration of domestic industry.

Table 37. Visible Trade 1969–74

	1969	1970	1971	1972	1973	1974
Exports: ($mn)						
Agroproducts	143	166	152	177	225	274
Fishproducts	220	338	336	279	149	219
Minerals	463	487	360	424	553	745
Other	40	59	45	45	114	282
Total	866	1050	893	943	1041	1520
Unit Price Index	100	119	97	109	128	351
Imports: ($mn)						
Food etc.	117	126	133	151	178	281
Consumer goods	32	25	31	34	43	683
Prodn. Inputs	246	247	361	375	417	
Capital goods	204	224	227	237	381	567
Total	603	622	752	797	1019	1531
Unit Price Index	100	122	108	97	194	277

Source: BCR (1974a.c)

Tariff policy has been somewhat overshadowed by direct embargoes and the fact that the state now accounts for all food imports, roughly half the capital goods, and roughly a third of industrial inputs imported. In any case, the rate of duty are not high, except on the residual consumer goods element and the rates themselves are basically those obtaining under the previous administration, apart from the extra 10% surcharge on all private imports imposed in 1969. The degree of 'effective protection' has not been calculated for Peru, but the value for industrial products is probably approximately double that of the 'ad-valorem' rates shown in table 38.[11]

Most of the banking system is now under state ownership and the controls over

Table 38. Import Tariff Structure (1973)

Item	Weight	Tariff
Food products	0.2	–
Other Consumer Goods	0.1	87%
Industrial Inputs	0.3	41%
Capital Goods	0.4	5%
Total	1.0	22%

Source: see Appendix I

the rest have been considerably strengthened[12]. As part of the stabilisation policy, primary emission and commercial credit has been restrained, only being increased to counteract the export fall in 1971. Bank credit expansion within the state sector, as we have seen, has been reflationary, however, but this is not shown by the conventional definition of liquidity. Table 39 also shows, incidentally, the relatively low and apparently decreasing importance of the use of demand deposits.

Table 39. Liquidity in the Economy: 1969–74

	1969	1970	1971	1972	1973	1974
(Billion soles)						
Currency	11.8	16.3	18.9	22.3	27.8	32.9
Demand Deposits	13.6	18.2	20.8	23.5	27.4	31.9
Total Liquidity	25.4	34.5	39.7	45.8	55.2	64.8
Ratio to money GNP	12.4%	14.5%	15.1%	15.6%	15.7%	(13%)

Source: BCR (1974c)

There has also been a policy to channel credit away from commerce and speculation towards productive activities:

> "The credit reform has been carried out in order to achieve the democratisation and regionalisation of credit, so that it is channelled adequately to all the active population, giving priority and preferential terms to the sectors of social interest and the most depressed regions of the country" (BCR 1974b)

As the table below shows, there has been some success in diverting credit extended by commercial and savings banks away from commerce[13] towards industry and construction. However, this is concentrated in the modern sector, and very little is getting through to peasant (i.e. foodcrop) producers. The reason for this is that the banking system as a whole, although it responds to government directives as to sectoral allocation, still operates on 'commercial' principles when granting individual loans. In other words, small enterprises (e.g. peasants, artisans) are considered a 'bad risk'.

Table 40. Distribution of Commercial Credit: 1967–74 (% of total)

<table>
<tr><th></th><th>1967</th><th>1970</th><th>1972</th><th>1974</th></tr>
<tr><td>Agriculture: foodcrops</td><td rowspan="2">10</td><td rowspan="2">7</td><td>1</td><td rowspan="2">4</td></tr>
<tr><td>other</td><td>4</td></tr>
<tr><td>Industry</td><td>25</td><td>35</td><td>40</td><td>37</td></tr>
<tr><td>Commerce</td><td>40</td><td>29</td><td>27</td><td>27</td></tr>
<tr><td>Construction</td><td>6</td><td>10</td><td>8</td><td>13</td></tr>
<tr><td>Other</td><td>19</td><td>19</td><td>20</td><td>19</td></tr>
</table>

Source: BCR (1974c)

The expansion of state credits in order to compensate for the imbalance of commercial lending has been also quite successful but the same pattern of concentration on the modern sector is repeated although it is here that one of the most effective ways of stimulating production in the traditional sector (and even 'modernising' it) should be. The regional distribution of commercial credit has shown some improvement, but it is still concentrated in Lima, although this reflects the existing spatial pattern of economic activity[14].

One of the aims of this credit policy was to restrict primary emission and thus restrain inflationary pressure. This was quite successful until 1973, when the combination of rising import prices and deficit financing raised prices by some 13%, to be followed by 20% in the next year, although food prices were held down by subsidised imports. Although this cannot be demonstrated statistically, it would appear that the result of this acceleration in prices has been to slightly worsen the income distribution, particularly affecting the urban poor, as those in the modern sector have been better able to protect their income levels.

Table 41. Price Indices (1969 = 100)

	Base year	1969	1970	1971	1972	1973	1974
Cost of Living*	1966	100	105	112	120	132	154
GDP Deflator	1963	100	107	111	116	132	158
Food: Retail*	1966	100	103	110	118	130	155
Wholesale	1960	100	95	96	117	133	...

Sources: BCR (1974a), BCR (1974c), ONEC (1975)
*in Lima

Finally, the maintenance of the exchange rate of the Sol over seven years without significant strain, even if it has required direct import restrictions, can be counted a significant success, although it is also a recognition of the fact that devaluation would not significantly affect the volume of exports or imports. Exchange reserves have been maintained at a historically high 'defensive' level of about five months' import equivalent.

We can conclude, then, that the objectives of short-term stabilisation policy have been achieved, but that the more severe underlying problems, particularly the continuing duality in the economy, have not been resolved.

5.3 Negotiations with Foreign Capital

The relationship between foreign enterprise and the state had been a leading issue in the events leading up to the 1968 coup, and the main element of the ownership reforms was logically the expropriation of a number of prominent foreign firms[15]. This, combined with the need for external public finance, means that negotiations between state and foreign capital are clearly central to the government's economic policy. The main problem in this bargaining process lies in the conflict between a desire to reduce dependence on the one hand and to acquire foreign cooperation on specific state projects on the other – in the face of opposition from international capital. Initially policy was somewhat unrealistic, as it anticipated both the reduction of this dependence and the renewed inflow of foreign capital. This is well illustrated in the 1971–75 Plan, where one of the main goals is stated to be the elimination

> "... of the subordination of the Peruvian economy to foreign centres of decision where actions originate which fundamentally affect the economic life of the nation and prevent an autonomous development process geared to the achievement of national objectives." (16)

but also a forecast of US$700 million in private capital inflows and US$1,100 millions in public capital, over the five-year period. In the event, a substantial reduction in foreign ownership of the means of production was achieved, but over the first four years, there was a net *outflow* of private capital and a net public inflow of only US$524 millions.

We shall start by giving a brief chronological survey of the main events in the 'bargaining calender'[17]. The 'players' are the Peruvian government on the one side, and on the other the representatives of international capitalism in the form of the US government, the World Bank, and the metropolitan commercial banks, as well as the multinationals themselves. The 'stakes' were, on the Peruvian side the threat of nationalisation and the offer of valuable mineral reserves, and on the side of foreign capital, finance for the external debt and cooperation in the resource extraction projects. In 1968, immediately after the coup, the IPC was expropriated and compensation witheld against excess profits expatriated in previous years. Although, at the time this was claimed by the Peruvian government to be an 'isolated incident'[18], 1969 saw a US suspension of sugar quotas and arms supplies, accompanied by an 'aid' freeze by the IBRD, which effectively denied Peru access to all but the most expensive international credit. The same year saw a dispute with the USA over fisheries boundaries, and the expropriation of ITT, Grace and the forclosure on unexploited oil and mining concessions. This did not, however, prevent negotiations over the Cuajone copper deposits with Southern Peru Copper continuing. In 1970, the Industrial Law was passed (providing for the labour communities, the phasing out of foreign ownership and control over the transfer of technology), the Banco Continental (owned by Chase Manhattan) taken over by the state and the US motor firms refused further production licenses. The financial freeze continued, as was only to be expected, but the accession of Allende in neighbouring Chile gave both valuable diplomatic support and an indication of the relative moderation of the Peruvian demands.

In the following year, 1971, relations with the USA eased, due principally to the world oil shortage and the value of the Peruvian concessions. The Peruvians, on their side, had gained most of their reform objectives, and had a greater need for finance. Thus the Mining Law was finally formulated (on generous terms), and the concessions established between PETROPERU and the oil multinationals – led by the major 'independent' Continental. In 1972, therefore, it was possible to renegotiate the external public debt, with the cooperation of the IBRD, even though mostly on the basis of Eurodollar finance on onerous terms. The events of these two years placed Peru in a relatively stronger position, so that in 1973 it was possible both to nationalise the fishing industry (half foreign owned) and the Cerro de Pasco on the one hand, and come to a final agreement on US$150 millions as compensation for all expropriated US property on the other. In 1974, the financing of the Cuajone project (which the state has underwritten) and the trans-Andean pipeline (PETROPERU) was finally settled, indicating the regained access to international finance – which was confirmed by the refinancing of the external debt in the spring of 1975.

The oil and copper projects are central to the future export pattern, and involve investments of the order of US$2,000 millions. After the relinquishment of the remaining unexploited mining concessions to the state in 1970 and the takeover of Cerro de Pasco in 1973, the SPC opencast copper mines at Toquepala (producing since the late 1950's) and Cuajone (due to start producing in 1977) are the only major private concessions, the Marcona iron ore operation having been nationalized in 1975.[19] Negotiations for Cuajone were started in 1969, and Peru insisted on control over refining, exports and foreign exchange resources, with a provision for eventual reversion of the operation to the state. SPC, in return required that the government arrange and underwrite project finance as well as guaranteeing capital recovery and adequate returns. Although the details are not all public[20], it would appear that much of the resulting Peruvian 'generosity' arose from the need to obtain the finance and settle the other items on the negotiating agenda, and indeed the matter was not settled until 1974. The control of refining and sales, however, means that MINEROPERU can secure any proportion of the profits desired in the future.

In 1971, the oil exploration and development concessions were finally signed between PETROPERU and the oil multinationals on a 'service contract' basis. This involves the companies incurring all investment costs on their own concessions (about two thirds of the total area, and rest being operated by PETROPERU directly) and in return retain a proportion of all crude found (about a half) the rest going to PETROPERU. This substitute for the normal method of income-tax is a Peruvian innovation and was calculated to provide a reasonable return to the concessionaires, but on the basis of the 1971 crude postings – so that the concessions are now enormously more profitable than anticipated. The Peruvian government is well aware of this dilemma, and one of two solutions will be adopted in 1978 when the oil begins to flow – either to impose a special tax or to set the tariff on the Trans-Andean pipeline (owned by PETROPERU and through which all the Amazonian oil must pass[21]) such as to recoup a greater proportion of the profit.

In the case of both copper and oil, it is reasonable to ask whether or not the Peruvian state enterprises could have carried out the projects themselves. The answer, although necessarily speculative, is probably affirmative. There is considerable mining experience in Peru, and open-cast exploitation is not technologically complex, while in the case of oil specialised sub-contractors can be obtained without too much difficulty[22]. The two constraints, however, were finance and the desire to commission the projects as quickly as possible. In the event, the decision to retain a third of the oil concessions and what is potentially the largest copper deposit (Cerro Verde) seems justifiable, albeit cautious.

An analysis of the balance of payments in recent years underlines these points about external capital movements as a whole. The visible trade balance[23] shows a consistent surplus that more than outweighs the net services item. The weight of interest payments on the public debt (see below) and private investment income outflows (these two are termed 'renta de inversiones' in the Peruvian balance of payments statistics), however, is large enough to turn the current account into payments statistics), however, is large enough to turn the current account into deficit. This last term is mainly accounted for by profit outflows[24], and although this is still large, the outflow has been reduced from the equivalent of 36% of declared post-tax profits in the economy as a whole in the period 1963–67 to 11% in 1970–73. It is capital account, however, that most concerns us here. The long-term capital inflow as a whole totalled some $564 million over the period 1969–73 and almost all of this is on public account, as there has been a net outflow of long-term private capital, mainly in the form of amortisation funds – in other words, the non-replacement of plant by foreign corporations – totalling some $65 million over the same period. There has also been a steady outflow of short-term capital ($200 million), probably the result of a reduction in suppliers' credits. Public borrowing has been expanded to cover this deficit and maintain the reserves at the historically high level of roughly six months' imports.

Table 42. Peruvian Balance of Payments: 1969–74 (US$ millions)

	1969	1970	1971	1972	1973	1974
Visible Trade Balance	221	335	159	133	108	–11
Services (net)	–37	–2	–67	–44	–77	n.a.
'Renta de Inversiones'						
Public	–37	–31	–48	–51	–66	–70
Private	–147	–117	–78	–70	–109	n.a.
Current Account	–	185	–34	–32	–144	n.a.
Long-term Capital						
Public	124	101	15	116	298	500
Private	20	–77	–43	–1	36	n.a.
Basic Balance	144	209	–62	83	190	n.a.
Short-term Capital	–56	21	–80	24	–109	n.a.
Monetary Movements*	–88	–230	142	–107	–81	n.a.

Source BCR (1974a), BCR
*including adjustments, errors etc.

The dominant feature in the capital account of the balance of payments is, as we have seen, government borrowing[25]. The composition of this borrowing is shown in table 43. In analysing the debt, a number of important factors must be taken into account. The first is the legacy of the past, in the form of a large debt inherited from the Belaunde regime, much of which was contracted so as to impose repayments at the end of that decade. In order to repay this debt, and without the possibility of recourse to 'soft' funding from the international agencies, it was necessary to borrow relatively short (i.e. three to five years) from commercial banks in Europe or America. In consequence, although the outstanding debt has mounted steadily, the net inflow has been very small, as the amortisation and interest payments have grown so rapidly. This position altered somewhat from 1974 onwards, as the major state investment projects worked their way through the system and access to the international agencies was gained. Some indication of the seriousness of the problem is given by the ratio of debt service to export revenue, and although

Table 43. External Public Debt: 1968–74 (US$ millions)

	1968	1969	1970	1971	1972	1973	1974
Amortisation	87	89	121	156	164	265	250
Interest	42	46	46	57	55	82	93
Servicing	129	134	167	213	219	347	343
Gross Inflow	186	221	190	184	285	574	990
Net Inflow	99	132	69	28	121	309	740
Outstanding Debt	737	875	945	997	1121	1430	2170
Ratio of Debt Service to Exports	15%	16%	16%	24%	23%	33%	22%

Source: BCR (1974b), BCR

this is not a wholly reliable indicator[26], its very high level does underline the problem, especially since the debt renegotiations of 1972 displaced the burden to 1976.

The central role of the USA and IBRD in the process of debt negotiation is worthy of note. In the period 1969–72, it was almost impossible for Peru to secure long-term funds, and even since that date most new finance has had to be raised on commercial markets at high rates and short repayment periods. In consequence, by the end of 1972, two-thirds of new finance and half of the outstanding public debt was in the form of suppliers credits. This 'freeze' is a good example of the way in which the IBRD acts as 'committee chairman' for international finance capital, and can effectively determine whether a particular country is to be considered creditworthy. The specific opposition was to the refusal to compensate IPC, the restrictions on direct foreign investment and the extension of state ownership; this opposition continued up to the 1972 'Consultative Group on Peru' meeting in Paris, where the IBRD claimed that the high level of foreign exchange reserves made further refinancing unnecessary.

There has been some diversification in sources of finance, and even some credit lines from the Soviet bloc, but the main source of funds remains, naturally, the metropolitan capital markets. This places a constraint on the freedom of action of the state in terms of policy in general and sources of import supply in particular.

Table 44. Sources of External Finance: 1966–74 (percent of total debt)

	1966	1969	1972	1974
Creditors:				
USA[a]	41	16	11	10
IBRD & IDB	18	19	19	21
Europe	29	38	40	42
Other	12	27	30	27

Source: ONEC (1973), BCR
(a) US Banks, USAID, ExImBank.

The main problems for the future, then, in relations with foreign capital, are the resolution of the terms on the oil and copper projects and the financing of the external debt. During 1973 and 1974, the volume of official finance increased markedly, as table 43 shows, responding to the new climate and the 'working through' of public investment projects, and in early 1975, some US$3,500 millions of credits were committed by the 'Paris Group' (see Chapter 7.4). The future possibilities are clouded, however, by the international financial depression and the unilateral expropriation of Marcona in July 1975. In the long run, however, the supply of external finance is dependent upon the implicit security of raw materials supplies to the capitalist economies.

5.4 Economic Strategy in a Dual Economy

Having examined the circumstances of policy on the domestic economy and foreign capital, we shall now turn to some of the fundamental issues on economic strategy which underly current policy-making. We shall examine three themes – the stagnation of food agriculture, the weakness in private investment and public finance. These three are, in fact, different aspects of the choice of economic strategy in a dual economy where the state does not even control the whole of the modern sector[28]. In discussing policy choices, we must be careful to avoid the Scylla of supposing all alternatives to be open on the one hand, and the Charybdis of excessive historical determinism on the other. The political circumstances constrain the policy field, because it is these circumstances that allowed the state intervention in the first place, but nonetheless the Peruvian government enjoys a considerable degree of freedom as a result of its relative autonomy from the domestic class structure.

The first theme is the most obvious consequence of the dual structure of the economy, which excludes the bulk of the population from the modern sector. As we have seen, the ownership reforms have been confined to this sector, and thus the problem remains. The resulting inequitable concentration of income affects both the urban and rural traditional sectors, but as far as the *economy* is concerned[29] the major problem is peasants as food producers. The situation, in styalised form, is roughly as follows: some 35% of the workforce is employed in food agriculture, producing about 80% of the domestic food requirements, which account for a third of personal consumption expenditure. The balance is imported, accounting for nearly a quarter of total imports and possibly as much as a half of the metropolitan food supply. This is, of course, a problem of long standing – according to the Minister of Agriculture, between 1960 and 1970 food crop output grew at 3.1% while demand grew at 4.6%, requiring ever-increasing imports of wheat, milk, vegetable oils and rice[30]. The corrolary of this is the declining share of peasant income in the national total which (when weighted by their declining proportion of workforce too) indicates that while the income distribution improved slightly towards the peasants up to 1970, the position has deteriorated somewhat since that date.

Policy response to this problem has been to attempt to avoid urban food shortages and rapid food price rises by importing food and subsidising it. This has been carried out by the public enterprise EPSA, which is also responsible for the buying in of certain domestic products (e.g. rice) at fixed prices[32]. As we have seen, the proportion of total credit devoted to food agriculture, as opposed to the agroexport

Table 45. Peasant Income Share: 1966–73

	1966	1969	1970	1971	1972	1973
Peasant Income as % of Nat. Income	11.2	11.3	12.0	10.0	8.8	8.5
Peasants as % of total workforce	32.7	31.2	30.7	30.2	29.7	29.2
Ratio of these	.34	.36	.39	.33	.30	.29
Index of Income per head	100	113	134	121	116	119

Source: footnote 31

complexes, is extremely small. Again, the major effort made to increase fertiliser production is geared almost entirely to the needs of the large irrigated units on the coast and not to the peasants who, indeed, have no means of purchasing it.

The essence of the problem is, in a sense, the absence of any agricultural policy except in the very short term – this being to keep prices down. A medium-term policy would require that peasant farm productivity be raised, and in turn both food supplies and the incomes of the rural poor increased. This would require more inputs and a greater retention of the surplus – either in the form of credits or higher prices[33]. In other words, a transfer of surplus from either the state or the urban consumer. To this would have to be added consistent production planning, marketing facilities (e.g. storage, transport) and extension services. In the longer term, however, the problem is the classical one of the relative weight to be given to agriculture and industry, and in consequence the spatial balance of incomes and population. It will probably require that both the arable land area be increased[34] and peasant production reorganised. The former is to some extent foreseen in the large coastal irrigation projects, but the second is a far more complex matter. Moreover, it is not entirely clear if the collectivisation of production (as opposed to services or marketing) would in fact improve output per hectare[35], and presumably a possible corrolary might well be peasant mobilisation on a political scale incompatible with the present system.

Private investment has been extremely low since 1968, being barely enough to

Table 46. Total Sectoral Credit Distribution: 1966–73 (billion soles)

	1966			1973		
	Private	State	Total	Private	State	Total
Industry	4.5	2.9	7.4	16.7	11.4	28.1
Agriculture	1.7	3.7	5.4	1.9	11.4	13.3
Construction	0.9	1.5	2.4	5.2	7.3	12.5
Other	8.6	0.6	9.2	18.7	2.1	20.8
Total	15.7	8.7	24.4	42.5	32.2	74.7

Source: BCR (1974b)

cover replacement[36]. This is contrary to government policy, which has been to reserve basic industry and exports to state ownership or strict control, but to allow 'reformed private enterprise' (i.e. with a labour community) to continue in the intersteces between state and cooperative enterprise. This is sustained not only by public statements but also by the provisions in the 1970 Industrial Law for tax incentives to investors in 'priority branches' of industry (i.e. those other than luxury consumer goods), the rapid expansion of credit through state banks and even the repayment conditions on the agrarian debt[37] – the particular objective being manufacturing. The result, however, has been disappointing. Once the expansion into excess capacity had been achieved by 1972, further growth was constrained and concentrated in consumer durables – the branch with the lowest priority – meaning that the structure of output is not developing adequately. Nonetheless, the private domestic savings rate has not declined much, it is just that more funds have been lent to the state. An attempt has also been made to widen the domestic capital market in order to encourage small savings and channel them towards industrial investment or government paper, but without much success, possibly because most of the available household savings are going into housing[38].

Table 47. Flow of Private Funds: 1969–73 (% of GDP)

	1969	1970	1971	1972	1973
Sources:					
Company Saving	10.4	11.7	12.8	12.6	14.4 (Company Saving and Household combined)
Household	1.3	2.6	1.7	0.6	
Foreign Finance	–3.3	–4.7	–0.4	–1.6	–2.5
Total Sources/Uses	8.4	9.6	14.0	11.6	11.9
Uses:					
Investment	8.2	7.9	7.7	7.7	8.2
Stockbuilding	1.0	0.5	2.4	1.3	0.8
Net lending to government	–0.8	1.2	3.8	2.5	2.9

Source: See Appendix III

The corollary of this weakness is that the bulk of the surplus in the modern sector is neither being used for capital accumulation nor is it in the hands of the state. The state has had to tap part of this surplus by borrowing and inflationary finance[39], and can exercise no real control over the production process either. A reflection of this latter point is the difficulty of controlling imported industrial inputs.

The logical policy alternative would seem to be (and have been) the nationalisation of key enterprises in the manufacturing sector[40], transferring to the state control over both profits and production. This would not present too much difficulty with respect to domestic capital, but the preponderant foreign element might have a greater power of resistance stemming from the external financial weakness of the government.

The third, and last theme is policy on external finance. Dependence upon direct foreign investment has certainly been reduced, but one of the chief weaknesses in negotiating the two extraction projects has been the shortage of external public finance, as the public debt has been substituted for other forms of capital inflow. Given a certain investment programme, borrowing to finance capital goods imports is essentially an alternative to the reduction of other import categories[41] and in effect, this means either food or industrial inputs, both of which are forms of consumption. It is an alternative, moreover, that only displaces in time the reduction in these consumption items (i.e. the debt service) so that analytically the problem can be reduced to the relative value of the 'consumption discount rate'[42] and the interest rate on the loans – and as with present rates of world inflation the latter is probably negative, the decision may seem correct. But this is to over-simplify the problem, the real question being whether the mounting external debt restricts the freedom of action of the government when negotiating with foreign enterprises. Foreign exchange availability is not a great technical problem in Peru and the difficulty is really centered on which groups should have their consumption cut in order to provide for capital accumulation, and foreign borrowing allows that decision to be deferred.

In sum, then, these three structural difficulties which have distorted government policy are all facets of the contradictions of a dual export-led economy. Long term planning of structural change should aim at resolving these difficulties – but their social implications may force the system into a different political frame of reference.

NOTES TO CHAPTER 5

1. This is not just a matter of censorship, but also a lack of public expertise in the topics and the 'hermetic' nature of the state itself. The problems with foreign capital do, however, cause much debate and are, naturally, the main concern of the international press.
2. We do not treat the Andean Pact as fully as we might in this study, but its present significance for Peru, beyond the investment rules already written into Peruvian law, is not yet great and there is some reason to fear that it will go the way of the LAFTA in any case. See Morawetz (1974) on technical aspects of the Pact.
3. BCR (1974b), author's translation
4. The annual 'Surveys' prepared by the Economic Commission for Latin America (Santiago, two years after year in question) are very useful.
5. This time it was not due to overfishing but rather the movement of warm currents into the anchovy grounds, which forced them out into the Pacific.
6. When reading the above table it should be remembered that 'manufacturing' includes the processing of primary export products, and therefore responds to trends in these as well. It would be useful to separate these out, but the BCR does not do this – see Appendix I, and also the discussion in Fitzgerald (1975).
7. See Chapter 3.3
8. See Appendix I on the indirect import component of manufacturing.
9. The share of other Latinamerican countries in Peruvian exports and imports is less than one tenth of the total – see Chapter 2.3
10. Appendix I. There is reason to believe some food imports are 'hidden' under other items.
11. There does not appear to exist a recent reliable study of effective protection for

Peruvian imports, and indeed there are no statistics of actual duty paid by import category. There are, of course, the *nominal* rates published by the Customs, and these are, with the weighted average for major commodity groups, given in INP (1975). However, there are exceptions for most capital goods, all state inputs – and overall the 10% surcharge on all private imports. These reduce the overall nominal duty rate of 45% on all imports to a realised rate (i.e. duty collected divided by imports cif) of 22% in 1973. The table in the text has been estimated as follows: (a) food – 0%; (b) capital goods – ½ public at 0%, half private at 10%; (c) non-food consumer goods – nominal rate; (d) industrial inputs – balance to make up the overall total.

12. See BCR (1974b)
13. Although borrowing firms usually cover both their own production and sales (i.e. commerce) so that the shift may be more apparent than real.
14. In 1971, 73% of deposits and 77% of loans were made in the capital (ONEC, 1973), indicating both the concentration on Lima and also the implicit transfer of funds from provinces. This is an old problem, although it is a slight improvement on the 1967 figures of 77% and 81%.
15. See Chapter 3.2
16. See INP (1971) p.15
17. See Hunt (1974), Ingram (1974)
18. Ingram (1974)
19. The somewhat precipitate transfer to the state in this case may cause further difficulties, but in any case, with the expansion of the state steel mills, the whole output would have been under state control by 1977.
20. There are several 'special' clauses among which are a concessionary exchange rate and exemption from import duty.
21. The strategic risk of using the Amazon route through Brazil to get the oil out, which would be far cheaper than the pipeline, was considered too great.
22. The example of Algeria is relevant in this context, as are the numerous consortia operating in the North Sea.
23. These figures are not the same as those in the full balance of payments due to slight differences in definition.
24. This does not include technology payments – but see Chapter 3.2
25. See footnote 23.
26. Referring as it does to a particular point in time and not to the period as a whole.
27. See Ingram (1974), and Payter (1974) on the worldwide activities of the World Bank, including a discussion of Belaunde's difficulties with the same institution.
28. As we shall see in Chapter 7, this problem is far from unique to Peru.
29. Another aspect of this is the narrowness of the domestic market caused by this concentration of income, a topic we take up later.
30. MinAg (1974). See also studies by Twomey (1973) and Millones (1973).
31. For this purpose, we define 'peasants' as the 'agricultores independientes' in the national accounts.
32. In 1973, the turnover of EPSA was equivalent to about 13% of total food sales in the economy, with a subsidy equivalent to 15% of turnover. See Chapter 4.
33. This is not a matter of increasing the marketed surplus as this appears to be already near its limit, but rather of production as a whole.
34. The allocation of arable land between food and export crops should be, in *economic* terms, a question of comparative advantage, as both are traded goods. In spite of the apparent advantage of export crops in this respect, the government has recently attempted to revive a decree first imposed some forty years ago that one third of all arable estates should be put under foodcrops.
35. See Barraclough (1973) and also Griffin (1974) on this point in a wider context, and Horton (1974) on the Peruvian case.
36. See Chapter 2.7. Depreciation runs at roughly 5% of GDP meaning that *net* capital formation in the private sector for 1969–73 has been only 2½% of GDP.
37. See Chapter 3.3

38. See Chapter 2.7, and also BCR (1974b).
39. See Chapter 4.3
40. E.g. the 'top 79' discussed in Chapter 2.6
41. For a general discussion of this point, see Kalecki (1972a)
42. See Little & Mirrlees (1968).

6

Economic Planning in Peru

6.1 The History of Planning in Peru

In order to provide a background to the planning system in Peru, a brief historical survey might be useful, as it provides a standard of comparison for the present system, particularly since the 1962–68 Peruvian planning system was very similar to that still obtaining in other Latinamerican economies. Economic planning as an explicit state activity[1] dates from the 1962–63 military regime which, in contrast to the 'laissez faire' approach of the previous government, felt that central co-ordination of the development effort in general and state economic activity in particular was needed. In 1962, the Instituto Nacional de Planificación was established within the Presidency of the Republic as a 'central planning office' with an initially expatriate technical staff and without executive power within the government. These origins were common to those of planning systems in many other Latinamerican countries, and a result of pressure from the 'aid donors' such as USAID and IBRD within the Alliance for Progress. This was not, of course, pressure for state control of the economy, but rather a requirement that in order to receive 'development assistance' then 'development projects' should be presented as part of 'development plans'.[2] This original objective should be borne in mind when evaluating the planning system between 1962 and 1968, although naturally much greater claims were made for it at the time. Planning during this period is discussed by Kilty (1967) in optimistic terms, and by Roel (1968) in more critical ones, reflecting the differing attitudes of an American and a Peruvian academic towards 'gradualismo reformista'.

The first Plan was not drawn up by the INP, but by the Central Bank in 1961 and was entitled 'Plan Nacional de Desarrollo Economico y Social del Peru 1962–71'.[3] It consisted of no more than a set of macro-economic projections for the economy (apparently unrelated either to an integrated aggregate model or to specific developments in particular sectors) and a list of government investment projects. There was no discussion of the means of implementation, nor of the social and structural difficulties in the economy, nor of how the plan was to be financed. However, it is of interest to note that very little state expansion was anticipated, although further incentives for private investors and a larger inflow of foreign capital were recommended. As Roel (op.cit., p.55) puts it:

> "The Plan . . . had only one objective – so that within the Alliance for Progress, Peru could be considered as one of the countries 'that had plans' ('que contaban con planes') and thus could solicit the financial services of the Alliance. The country was hardly aware of the Plan, but that was not a

> matter for preoccupation, for nobody in the Government seriously meant to implement anything resembling integrated planning."[4]

The Plan had little impact, not only because of the limited state control over the economy, but rather because the Belaunde government was installed in 1963 and had different goals. Despite the reformist objectives of the Belaunde regime, the fiscal and budgetary reorganisation of 1963 and the expansion of state activity in infrastructure and development finance, a new plan was not drawn up until 1966 – the 'Plan de Desarrollo Economico y Social 1967–70' (INP, 1966).

This was a considerable improvement over the first Plan, particularly in the diagnosis of the problems of the economy and the internal consistency of the Plan itself. The problems diagnosed included the duality of the economy, underemployment, concentration of ownership, excessive control by foreign enterprises and spatial imbalance in the economy. The means for resolving these problems, however, did not correspond to the diagnosis. The internal consistency of the projections was improved by the use of macro-economic models[5], but these did not reflect the diagnosis either, being based on conventional 'two-gap' and 'capital-output' methods. Both these improvements represent the growing technical competence of the INP during the period, and it was wholly responsible for the second Plan. The main difficulty, however, was that there was no provision for the implementation of the forecasts in the Plan, while the public investment programme was no more than a collection of projects proposed by the various ministries and unconnected to the aggregate projections. As Roel (op.cit. p.180) points out:

> "The Plan is no more than a guide which expresses the trends which the Government intends to follow, because no Minister, nor the President of the Republic, nor the Congress, base their decisions on it."

Moreover, the severe external and fiscal disequilibria of 1967, followed by the events of 1968, meant that the second Plan was never implemented.

This poor record of planning in the 1961–68 period is not surprising, because the economic role of the state at that time was to support rather than control the private sector. Its task, therefore, was to respond to the sectoral requirements of domestic and foreign capital (e.g. roads, irrigation), provide cheap finance (the bancos de fomento) and raise loans abroad. The Plans were really only drawn up to satisfy the 'aid agencies'[6] and to sustain the image of the government as 'reformista' at home – but even at these limited tasks they were not very successful.

The first plan implemented under the Gobierno Revolucionario de la Fuerza Armada was the 'Plan del Perú 1971–75' (INP, 1971) drawn up in 1970 and the second is the 'Plan Nacional de Desarrollo 1975–78', formulated in 1974, the content and implementation of which are the subject of this chapter. The main differences from previous plans are two. Firstly, the objectives cover changes in ownership as well as economic growth, within the context of greater integration of the economy and a reduction in external dependency. Secondly, state control over the economy has been so extended as to make a considerably greater degree of implementation possible – in most cases by direct public sector action. It is these changes, which are the result of developments in the political economy as a whole, combined with greater realism in the diagnoses, rather than the improvements in techniques and models, that represent the main step forward in Peruvian planning.

In this chapter[7] we shall examine the organization of the planning system since

1968, and then turn to the processes of macroplanning and microplanning before analysing the 'concrete manifestation of the plan' – capital formation in the public sector.

6.2 The Organization of Planning

One of the major tasks of the Peruvian state as 'national entrepreneur' is to rationalize the allocation of resources, and central to this is the Sistema Nacional de Planificación (national planning system), the function of which is constantly stressed by the government[8]. One of the first acts of the new regime was to strengthen the planning system and to give the INP considerable executive powers.

The planning system as a whole is basically made up of the Instituto Nacional de Planificación, with ministerial status within the Presidency, and the Oficinas Sectoriales de Planificación (sectoral planning offices) within each ministry, the whole providing plans for the approval of the COAP as chief policy-making body. These plans are of three main types. *First* there are the Planes de Desarrollo (development plans) themselves, that is, the 1971–75 Plan and the 1975–78 Plan. For these, special commissions are formed in the previous year to establish objectives and consider intersectoral issues (e.g. technology, population) as well as the sectoral commissions (based on the sectoral planning offices) to coordinate the programmes with the INP. These Development Plans are framed within the general long-term strategic objectives of the government[9], and cover topics such as ownership reform and structural change as well as production and investment. *Second* there are the Planes Bienales (biennial plans) which contain production forecasts, detailed public investment budgets, lists of projects and state enterprise programmes and upon which the financial requirements can be calculated. These biennial plans are the responsibility mainly of the INP, working with the sectoral planning offices. *Third* there are the Planes Economicos (economic plans) which are in fact a combination of updated macroeconomic forecasts and the operating budgets of the ministries for the next fiscal year, and are mainly drawn up by the Ministry of Finance. In practical terms, the Development and Biennial Plans are the crucial ones, as the annual plans are for too short a period and are dominated by previous decisions on resource allocation.

The INP employs some two hundred planners, and these are organized in three 'areas' which deal respectively with macroplanning and social strategy, microplanning and projects, and external economic relations and technology transfer. To these is attached a research division, and the whole is coordinated by the 'dirección técnica' which provides the minister's own staff and edits the reports to COAP. Apart from the head office in Lima, the INP has four regional offices – ORDECENTRO (Huancayo), ORDESUR (Arequipa), ORDENORTE (Chiclayo) and ORDEORIENTE (Iquitos) – dealing with the Central, South, North and Amazon regions respectively[10]. The INP is also in close contact with the sectoral planning offices in each ministry, which are often staffed by INP 'graduates'.

The INP has a number of tasks that make up its overall function as the central planning agency. The first is the obligation to draw up the aggregate, sectoral and project programmes, and to monitor their execution, a function we shall discuss in the next two sections. The second is to formulate the biennial budgets and to screen all public investment projects requiring finance from the central government. The third is to act as a secretariat to the COAP, supplying information and advice as a form of 'cabinet office'. The fourth is to provide a coordinating element between the various ministries and agencies at a regional level. These functions complement one another in an interesting way. The primary, planning function is given weight both by the direct access to the central decision-making body and by the control over public investment funds. This point is of some importance, because it gives the INP some power over the ministries, which could not be assured by merely administrative dispositions[11]. The regional planning offices gain local weight from their direct contact with the Presidency, and also because there is no other 'multisectoral' representative of the government at a regional level apart from the military. These regional offices, however, have not gained great importance due to the slow progress in decentralising the public sector as a whole.

Although the entire public sector is involved in the planning process (the state enterprises through their 'parent' ministries, and these linked to the INP through the OSP's), neither the private sector nor workers' organisations nor the populace as a whole are formally consulted in the policymaking process. There are no 'joint commissions' of any kind, although naturally the executive agencies have informal contact with private capital (particularly the major enterprises) on a day-to-day basis. This partly reflects the lack of articulated proprietors' or workers' organizations capable of presenting coherent alternatives to government policy, but is also due to the military concept of how the state should be organized.[12]

Finally, we must make a brief comment on the planners themselves.[13] They are a generally young and well-trained body of technocrats, mostly educated as economists, engineers (often with a second degree in economics) and sociologists, these last gaining ground against the remnants of the 'lawyer-bureaucrat' group. The level of commitment is high, although there is some lack of experience and first-hand knowledge of the economy, partly counterblanaced by an eagerness to learn and experiment. Of particular interest is the shift in economic thought among the planners, away from 'North American' towards 'European' schools of thought – a move from 'economic science' towards 'political economy' and from 'economic efficiency' towards 'structural change' – in response to the changing political attitude to the development problems of Peru. Another relevant indicator is the critical attitude towards outsiders in general, and towards foreign enterprise and 'experts' in particular.

6.3 The Macroplanning System

The macroplanning system is based on sectoral estimates of production, investment and employment provided by the OSP's, these being coordinated and made consistent by the INP. The basis of these forecasts varies from one sector to another. For example, in mining, petroleum and fishing the forecasts of output, exports and investment requirements are quite good (natural resource conditions allowing) because production is organised in large units under state control. In industry, the forecasts of final output are based on extrapolation of demand and then simple input coefficients applied to derive requirements for heavy industry. In agriculture and services, however, although the forecasts are reasonably reliable for products organised in large units (i.e. sugar, banking) those for the remainder of the sectors are pure conjecture. Once these estimates of production and employment in each sector have been fitted together, import requirements are derived from the input-output system. Public investment budgets are derived directly from the microplanning system (see 6.4 below) and the visible balance of trade from the sectoral export and import forecasts. From this trade balance, plus the debt servicing and the external finance requirements (see 6.4 below) the overall balance of payments position is calculated. This methodology is applied to both the Development Plans and the Biennial Plans, and contains an element of internal adjustment through the aggregation of sectoral output and employment forecasts to give total domestic product and employment which is then fed back to the OSP's in order that the demand forecasts be brought into line.

This methodology for macroeconomic planning has three main difficulties. First, it is basically a method of *forecasting* output in the modern sector, and although these do correspond to broad sectoral priorities, they are not derived from any 'bill of goods' in terms of future consumption or investment patterns. Second, there is no exploration of alternative sets of projections, particularly the effects of different export and public investment levels on the economy as a whole. Third, the aggregate estimates are not integrated into the sectoral programmes except through the original output and investment forecasts fed up from the OSP's. The INP is in the process of remedying this by building a computer model of the Peruvian economy so that some form of iteration can be applied as well as sensitivity testing and analysis of internal consistency. Unfortunately the models used[14] are somewhat 'conventional' and do not correspond to the nature of the Peruvian economy.

Having said this, it is only fair to suggest how an appropriate model might be constructed. The main elements would probably be:

a) Each sector divided into modern and traditional sub-sectors, on the basis of an estimate of the workforce and output from each sector, using the 1963 and 1973 economic censuses. The modern sector is the dynamic growth element, with the traditional sector dependent upon it and absorbing the bulk of the workforce.

b) The growth of the modern sector is now a function of exports on the one hand and public investment on the other. Exports are determined exogenously, mainly by a series of key projects outside the model.[15] Public investment is an explicit variable in the system, within the financial constraints, based on the lists of feasible projects.

c) Food agriculture is forecast separately, and the labour force allocation derived from the requirements of the modern sector (under various different strategies for capital-intensity) on the one hand and the balance between urban traditional and peasant population on the other, along the lines discussed in Chapter 2.2.

d) Consumption demand for basic products should be programmed on the basis of income distribution and the relevant price and income elasticities on an aggregate system.[16] Domestic output of food is forecast independently, and so imported shortfalls can be estimated, but as all other consumer goods are produced domestically, in the modern sector, this gives the manufacturing output plan. From this the estimates of intermediate production and import requirements can be derived.

Naturally this model would be used as the basis of sectoral forecasts to be used in the microplanning process, the results of which would be fed back into the aggregate plan on an iterative basis – although the number of times that this can be done is severely limited by the administrative complexity involved.

A major difficulty with the present form of macroplanning (and this is a problem with the Peruvian system of state intervention as a whole, as we have seen in Chapter 4) is not one of methodology but lies in the fact that it is based on production and not on resources. In consequence, two vital aspects of development tend to be ignored. The first is the problem of how the plan is to be financed – in other words the acquisition of sufficient proportion of the surplus to provide for capital accumulation. The result is to let the external debt 'take the strain' with effects that we have observed in the previous chapter. The use of foreign exchange as a whole should be programmed with consumption uses as a residual, and corporation tax and state enterprise profits considered as an explicit variable. The second is that employment, and thus the income distribution, is an output from rather than an input to the planning process. The derivation of employment programmes from sectoral agencies (which are interested in production and investment) rather than setting employment and income targets for different groups initially means that these objectives tend to fall by the wayside.

It might be of some interest to examine the outcome of the 1971–75 Plan now that it is more or less completed, but it should be remembered that this plan was conceived within the general economic 'holding operation' during the reform years. As we can see from the table below, growth in the agricultural sector was well below that planned – in fact a growth more rapid than that of population had been forecast, in the expectation that the food supply position would not deteriorate – and very little was done to help non-export producers, which kept growth down to the historical trend. The fishing sector, of course, collapsed in 1973 for unforseeable ecological reasons, which is why even the relatively cautious value in the Plan was an overestimate. The mining sector was affected by strikes which were, in a sense, the result of unfulfilled hopes raised by government declarations. As a result, the growth of these primary sectors was well below that planned, and so GDP growth, although quite high, fell below the forecast, pulling down industry and services with it. As far as the sectoral shares in output at the end of the period are concerned, the poor forecasts of the primary sectors and the relatively better one for industry lead to the latter ending up with a larger share than planned.

In consequence, the internal migratory drift was considerably greater than planned; indeed, one of the objectives of the Plan was to decelerate the process of urban growth. This was slightly counterbalanced by the fact that the 1972 population census[17] revealed that the population growth rate for the previous decade was lower (2.9%) than that forecast (3.1%). Also, the targets with respect to the reduction in underemployment do not appear to have been met – although the basis of the estimates in the Plan is not clear and no subsequent ones are available.

Turning to the investment programme, we have already noted how the planned inflow of foreign capital was not forthcoming and the reasons for the weakness in domestic savings. The Plan realistically forecast a relatively low level of domestic capital formation in the private sector, but overestimated the public investment level by a wide margin. The latter was due partly to the difficulty in raising foreign finance but mostly to the delay in implementing a number of major projects.

This, finally, leads us on to the question of how the aggregate plan is

Table 48. Outcome of the 'Plan del Peru 1971–75'

	Structure (% GDP)			Growth Rate (% p.a. 1971–75)	
	1970	1975			
		Plan	Actual*	Plan	Actual
Agriculture	14.5	12.4	12.6	4.2	2.0
Fishing	2.1	1.9	1.4	4.8	–0.6
Mining	6.8	6.3	7.1	5.7	3.2
Industry	20.9	26.0	27.4	12.4	9.7
Other	55.7	53.3	51.5	6.6	5.7
GDP	100.0	100.0	100.0	7.5	6.2

Source: INP (1971a), INP.
*The 'actual' figure for 1975 is in fact the forecast made at end 1975.

Table 49. Investment under the 'Plan del Peru'

	1970	1974		Growth Rate 1971–74	
		Plan	Actual	Plan	Actual
Gross Fixed Capital Formation: (bn soles)					
Private	19.0	23.4	26.0	7.0	8.2
Public	10.9	33.8	25.2	38.7	26.0
Total	29.9	57.3	51.2	18.9	14.4
Share of GDP	12.4%	18.1%	17.0%.		

Source: INP (1971a), INP.

implemented. In the sense of consistent measurement of 'target fulfillment' and executive action to rectify deviations, this is not done, simply because the government does not control final output directly. What is done is to provide, through the internal 'Informes Trimestrales' (quarterly reports), as recent a check as possible on production and allow the matter to be raised with the relevant minister at cabinet level and also to permit the next biennial plan to be adjusted accordingly. Unfortunately the poor statistical services weaken the process. In effect, therefore, the main monitoring and supervision system is on microplanning, as we shall see in the next section.

6.4 The Microplanning System

The system of microplanning is concerned primarily with public sector investment programmes, and as it is these that form the basis of government restructuring of the economy, it is here that the 'cutting edge' of planning should be found. As we shall see, considerable progress has been made since 1968 to improve the microplanning system, which before 1969 had been no more than the accumulation of projects proposed by the ministries, and the main deficiencies that remain relate to the nature of state intervention in the economy.

The present organisation of project appraisal is complex, but of some interest in illustrating the operation of an important aspect of development administration. A project concept is conceived in a ministry, agency or public enterprise, and submitted in outline to the sectoral planning office (OSP) in the relevant ministry, for approval in relation to sectoral strategy. Once this has been approved as a reasonable possibility, it is entered in a list of 'pre-feasibility' studies sent to the INP, and a full feasibility study initiated. This feasibility study is carried out within the agency (often using outside experts contracted for the purpose) and if not, commissioned from a firm of domestic or foreign consultants. On completion, this study is checked by the OSP for technical and commercial feasibility and for conformity to sectoral planning objectives[18]. If the project requires central government finance it is then passed to the INP; this covers all projects of any importance, as only the smallest are included in the operating budgets. The INP then subjects the study to an economic cost-benefit analysis in order to establish the economic viability of the project on the one hand and its conformity with overall development objectives. Projects are then either rejected, sent back to the ministry for reformulation or granted provisional acceptance.[19] Once accepted, it is provisionally entered in the draft of the Plan Bienal and passed to the relevant financing body.

In the case of foreign finance, which is normal if imported equipment is required, the relevant body is the COFIDE[20], which is responsible for channelling all foreign finance to state projects, and which establishes the best (i.e. cheapest, given the range of suppliers) source of foreign finance, as well as commenting upon the financial structure of the project. In the case of domestic finance, the project goes to the Dirección de Crédito Público (the Directorate of Public Credit, a department of the Ministry of Finance) for clearance and inclusion in the domestic borrowing requirements. The DCR also records external committments contracted by the COFIDE, and as the majority of projects have elements of domestic and foreign finance the two institutions are involved on most occasions. The project finally goes to the 'projects sub-committee' of the COAP for a final decision, the ministers from the INP, the Ministry of Finance and the relevant Ministry attending. The project, if finally approved, is included in the Plan Bienal and cleared for execution.

Once the project is approved, its implementation is the primary concern of the agency concerned, and is usually carried out by a private contractor[21]. Meanwhile, the INP keeps a quarterly check on project implementation through both the OSP and its own regional offices. Details of project progress are recorded on a punched-card system, which is used both for programming expenditure on existing projects and warning the projects sub-committee if special action is needed.

Needless to say, major projects tend to accumulate their own 'pressure groups' among the beneficiaries and also within the administration, so that once under way to the feasibility stage they are very difficult to stop or even to modify. In administrative terms, the problem is felt to lie in the fact that the projects reach the INP 'too late in life' and are difficult to stop, or where they blatantly fail to conform to development objectives, to reformulate without rejection. The policy response[22] to this has been to recently set up a system by which the INP intervenes at the prefeasibility stage, ensuring that a larger range of project alternatives are considered, aims such as employment, income distribution, regional balance and exchange shortage can be included, and unsuitable projects 'nipped in the bud'. Moreover, the use of outside consulting firms is to be reduced to the essential minimum, so as to build up an 'in-house' capability. The first step in this direction to establish central control over project generation is in the organisation of the Social Property sector.

The methodology used by the INP for the cost-benefit analysis of public investment projects is based on that worked out by the ECLA nearly two decades ago[23]. The evaluation at market prices supplied by the OSP is adjusted to deduct tax payments or subsidies and a discount rate of 10% applied[24] at constant prices to derive the Net Present Value, which must be positive to achieve acceptance.[25] Then, foreign exchange items are adjusted for a 'shadow rate or exchange' (50 soles per US$),[26] and if the project still has a positive net present value it is accepted. A check is also made on the commercial and financial analysis of the project, to assure adequate pricing, cash flow and so forth. Some headway has been made with the introduction of sensitivity testing for key project variables (e.g. export prices) although not, as yet, uncertainty analysis.

The method has some shortcomings. First, there is an inconsistency in treatment of shadow prices; on the one hand a shadow wage rate should be applied if employment objectives are to be considered, taking into account the alternative employment of unskilled labour used on state projects, the effect upon the balance of savings and consumption in the economy, and the supply of wagegoods – a suggested methodology for which is suggested in Fitzgerald (1975). On the other hand, the shadow price for foreign exchange should be applied to *all* traded goods and the traded component of non-traded goods, rather than just the direct import or export component of the project.[27] Further consideration might well be given to the ex-ante programming of the foreign exchange allocation as a whole as this is now completely under government control, and indeed nine-tenths of exports and half of imports are generated by state enterprises. However, the main problems do not lie here in the cost-benefit analysis method itself, but rather in the project appraisal system.

First, there is no formal budgeting system within the sectoral allocations, such as might be provided by the method of ranking projects according to the ratio of net present value to the capital budget cost[28]. In practice, the projects with positive net present value tend to take up the available budget on a 'first come first served' basis. This was not too important in the 1969–73 period as there was a comparative shortage of feasible projects, but is now becoming a major difficulty. Second, although projects with traded output (i.e. import-substitution or export projects) can be valued exogenously in terms of international prices, those with non-traded output (e.g. power, steel, roads, water etc.) which still make up a large part of public investment, have no marginal value and decisions must be made on a cost-minimisation basis. In this case, the output decisions should form part of the central planning system and not be left to the individual operating agencies.

As in the case of macroplanning, the data base[29] for project analysis is very poor. In particular, there is a need for more information on technical parameters (e.g. demand elasticities, input coefficients), larger lists of project possibilities, and above all the local operating conditions which determine project 'success'. In this area, the recent strengthening of the research division and regional offices of the INP should help.

As we cannot enter in operating details of individual projects[30], we shall turn to the experience of resource allocation in the public sector in a more aggregate manner, particularly in order to establish the extent to which this allocation has changed under this government. First, some comments on the relative size of projects might be useful. In 1973, the public sector had three thousand investment projects under way, of which only 150 had a programmed investment of more than 50 million soles[31] but these accounted for some 70% of total public fixed investment in 1973. Of these, ten projects accounted for 45% of that total, and are shown in the list below, giving a good idea of the microplanning priorities. The reduced number of significant projects means that the monitoring system discussed above does not become excessively burdensome in administrative terms.

Table 50. Key Development Projects in 1973[32]

Project	Agency	Total Investment* (soles billion)
Talara Fertilizer Complex	PETROPERU	2.29
Mantaro Hydroelectric Plan	ELECTROPERU	1.72
Amazon Oil Exploration	PETROPERU	3.68
Other Oil Operations	PETROPERU	2.38
Chira-Piura Irrigation	Min.Agriculture	5.30
Talara Refinery	PETROPERU	2.29
Cerro Verde Copper Mine	MINEROPERU	3.60
Ilo Copper Refinery	MINEROPERU	2.33
Water Supply Programme	Min.Housing	3.82
School Centres Programme	Min.Education	1.50

Source: INP (1974b)
*as estimated in 1974

One of the key elements in the 1971–75 Plan was the reorientation of public investment away from infrastructure towards productive projects, particularly exports and heavy industry as well as social services:

> "The allocation of this (public) investment will be radically different from that carried out by the Public Sector in the past. . . . in the period 1960–67 public investment was directed fundamentally towards physical infrastructure, while in the 1971–75 period the principle investments will be made in minerals and industry" (INP, 1971a, p.23 – author's translation).

Table 51 shows the result of this decision, in terms of the sectoral shares of capital formation. As can be seen the structure has changed, broadly in line with the Plan, the main shift being from transport to mining – from roads to copper and oil. The deviation from the Plan is due to two factors – the acceleration of the oil exploration programme and the delays in implementing the manufacturing projects,[33] particularly in the metals sector. In aggregate terms, the latest complete results

Table 51. Gross Fixed State Capital Formation by Sector: 1960–74

Sector	1960–67 (actual)	1971–75 (plan)	1971–72 (actual)	1973–74 (budget*)
Agriculture	8	8	9	13
Transport	30	16	15	11
Mining, Oil	–	16	11	27
Industry	14	25	15	19
Fishing	–	5	2	3
Other	48	30	48	27
Total	100	100	100	100

Source: INP (1971a), INP (1973b), INP (1974b).
*as of early 1974.

(1973) show a functional allocation of total public sector fixed investment between 'economic' (63%), 'social' (22%) and 'general' (15%) activities.

The other key strategy in the 1971–75 Plan was that public investment should be geared towards regional development more than in the past. The long-term nature of this task was recognized, and neither past investment by region nor specific targets were set. The 1971–72 public investment figures do, however, have a regional breakdown, which is shown in the table below. As can be seen, the greater part of public investment is specific to the regions, although the low proportion going to local government should be noted also. However, two large items are to some extent misleading – about half the 'Norte-Central Government' figure is reconstruction after the 1970 earthquake, and much of the 'Centro-State Enterprise' figure is in fact hydro-plant for Lima. The important point, however, is that most of the development projects are 'location-specific' (e.g. oil, mining, irrigation) already and although the regions benefit, are all 'modern sector' developments, so they do not do much to raise the incomes of those in the rural-traditional sector. The industrial programming since 1971–72 includes the concentration of new 'metalmecanica' and transport equipment plant in Trujillo (Norte), cement production in Selva and Sur, and both electrification and tourist facilities in the southern Sierra. These should tend to rectify the position somewhat, and the giant irrigation projects in Chira-Piura (Norte) and Majes (Sur) will expand rural employment and food production – but again these correspond to the modern sector.

The issue of external finance is relevant to the microplanning process in two ways. First, although much of the new foreign debt has, until recently, been contracted to refinance the old[34], the rapid expansion in 1973 and 1974 was due to the raising of supplier credits against imports of equipment for public investment projects. Second, the Peruvian planners and 'aid negotiators' see the 'project list' as a means of borrowing foreign exchange *in general*, by constructing a fixed list and then inviting 'donors' to choose from that list. In this way the financing country has less effect on the projects, and Peru's 'own' foreign exchange is released for other purposes[35].

Table 52. Regionalisation of State Capital Formation 1971–72

Region	Central Govt.	State Enterprise	Local Govt.	Total
Norte (north)	20	7	2	29
Sur (south)	9	2	2	13
Oriente (Amazon)	5	4	1	10
Centro (centre)	7	13	1	21
'Regions'	41	26	6	73
Lima-Callao	4	12	3	19
'National'*	6	2	–	8
Total	51	40	9	100

Source: INP (1973b)
*i.e. defence etc.

However, the microplanning system as described above has the defect of allowing the debt to accumulate in a somewhat haphazard way as the foreign element in the project is arranged (by COFIDE) *after* the project has been approved by the INP, and for this latter it is not an explicit decision criterion. In practice, the designers of the project, who want the 'best' equipment and rapid delivery[36], tend to favour foreign suppliers by appropriate specification in the original design. The policy of allowing high foreign exchange content in projects generating foreign exchange themselves (i.e. import-substitution or exports) does counteract this slightly, but it might be more advisable to programme a limit on the external debt and then allocate this between branches or projects. For the period 1974–76, projects worth some US$3.40 billion were listed for foreign finance, of which $1.78 billion was the import component and it was hoped to raise $2.03 billion in foreign finance.[37] About a third of this was for industrial projects, where the need for imported equipment and technology appears to be greatest.

The microplanning system, then, has shown considerable improvement, and is now the most effective part of the Sistema Nacional de Planificación. In particular, the channelling of projects through the national planning office (with its 'weapon' of budgetry control), the rapid implementation of projects by the new state enterprises and the monitoring system are worthy of mention. However, it reflects the mode of state intervention in the economy as a whole – the priority given to rapid accumulation in the modern sector, rather than the raising of income in the traditional sector – and the lack of control over the production of domestic consumer goods. In consequence, the 'faults' we have mentioned (such as the lack of employment criteria, the failure to integrate final production requirements and the regional problem) are the outcome of the process itself, and to 'reform' them is not just an administrative matter.

6.5 Problems in Planning

Having examined the Peruvian economic planning system in some detail, we can briefly comment on the system as a whole. In general, it reflects the nature of state intervention in the economy, as in any other country, and is not a separate phenomenon, but rather a manifestation of that intervention. The 'shortcomings' are not, therefore, primarily a question of administrative reform or better techniques (although there is clearly much to be done here) but rather the result of a divergence between the implicit and explicit objectives of planning – between the economic function of the state and the expectations of 'optimal planning' on the part of observers. We have seen how planning is organized primarily on a microeconomic basis (because of the importance of public investment) with the central planning office (INP) selecting projects from those proposed by the operating agencies within guidelines established by the COAP. We have also seen how this system leaves out aspects such as the programming of domestic consumer goods supply, the generation of employment, regional balance, and the mounting external debt. Similarly, the macroeconomic planning system appears to err in setting the balance between modern industry and traditional agriculture on the one hand, and in not allowing for resource inputs – particularly public finance and employment – on the other.

However, this arises from the mode of state intervention in the Peruvian economy. The state does not control food supply or final manufacturing. The state enterprises[38] have specific production objectives, and they naturally attempt to achieve these in an 'enterprise' manner, and as they are all in the modern sector and receive the bulk of investment funds, it is not surprising that the traditional sector suffers. Nonetheless, within the current mode of intervention, much more could be done about limiting the foreign component of investment and strengthening industrial linkages (which two amount to almost the same thing) if not about employment criteria and regional balance.

In the matter of organization and technique, the full implementation of the prefeasibility system will require a strengthening of the regional offices of the INP and greater expertise among planners about the technical details of production, so as to evaluate project proposals more critically. We have already considered some suggestions as to how the macroeconomic model might be improved, and as to how the project appraisal technique might be made more consistent with development objectives. We have also noted the extreme poverty of the data base for planning, especially with respect to 'structural' characteristics such as the composition of demand, firm size, income distribution, sectoral capabilities and production costs.

Finally, after these (hopefully constructive) comments it must be pointed out[39] that the national planning system in Peru appears to be the most effective in continental Latin America, and compares favourably with any in the non-socialist underdeveloped world.

NOTES TO CHAPTER 6

1. Some form of planning, in the sense of objectives and coordinated action to achieve them, is implicit in all budgeting, and thus existed in embryonic form in the 'Presupuesto de la Republica' and possibly in the activities of the major ownership groups in the private sector.
2. ECLA (1967)

3. BCR (1961). Indeed the preface to this Plan is a letter to the Organisation of American States from the Treasury Minister pointing out that Peru had now fulfilled its obligations in this respect.
4. The distinction between 'que contaban con planes' and 'planificadas' should not be lost.
5. Thorbecke and Condos (1966). Their model, for all its statistical and sophistication and mathematical elegance, bears no relation whatsoever to the political economy of Peru.
6. This is not to suggest that the international agencies were deceived, but rather that they had their own 'constituencies' to convince. On this see Griffin & Enos (1972).
7. The author's work in Peru during 1974 was with the INP, but it is not possible to go into operational details, for reasons of confidentiality.
8. INP (1972a)
9. See Chapter 1.3
10. INP (1972b)
11. This is considered by ECLA (1967) to be the key weakness in Latin American planning generally.
12. Although of course from the planner's point of view the less of this there is the better!
13. This is necessarily a personal opinion, but it has been corroborated by other observers, and bears mentioning.
14. INP (1973d) gives the simulation model used, which was constructed with the help of the University of Pennsylvania. The model is based on regression analysis of the national accounts, and treats the economy as homogeneous, without consideration of duality or differences between production sectors. Nor is there any consideration of the labour market, the balance of payments or income distribution.
15. This would be an important area for sensitivity testing and risk analysis, particularly to examine the destabilizing consequences of project delays and price variations on international commodity markets.
16. That is, not just by the OSP's, as is the present practice.
17. INP (1973)
18. The OSP for the Ministry of Agriculture has issued, for example, a methodology for allocation priority to economic and social objectives – MinAg (1972).
19. The measurement of this process is not possible, as most 'bad' projects are held back through informal consultation.
20. See Chapter 4.3
21. It is possible that an Empresa Nacional de Construcción will be set up to carry out public works directly. This would control the 'leakage of surplus' to the private sector, while ensuring the use of local materials and employment generation.
22. 'Proyecto-Ley de Estudios de Pre-Factibilidad para la Inversión Pública' (INP, Lima, July 1974).
23. UNIDO (1958)
24. The origin of this figure is not clear, although it has become conventional in international agencies to use a figure of this magnitude.
25. Or where the internal rate of return exceeds the discount rate, which is equivalent when a single project is considered.
26. This is based on a 20% markup, itself roughly corresponding to the ratio of domestic to international prices – the mean tariff rate. See INP (1975)
27. Little & Mirrlees (1968)
28. Sometimes known as the 'cost-benefit ratio'. For a definition and discussion of capital programming in the public sector, see Millward (1971).
29. See Appendix IV
30. Due to the author's position as an adviser on this topic. In fact, an extremely interesting analysis could be made by tracing reports of the progress of large projects through the press.
31. US$1.2 millions
32. The only really large projects missing from this list (because they did not involve large

outlays in 1973) are the Majes irrigation scheme and the Michiquillay copper mine.

33. The difference to the 1960–67 industrial investment is the weight given to productive projects such as 'metalmecanica', transport equipment, agricultural machinery and mineral refining.
34. See Chapter 5.3
35. That is, an explicit recognition of 'fungibility'. See Chapter 5.3
36. Local suppliers tend to be slow, offer shorter credit terms, and not to have the same technical quality – but it is difficult to see how domestic suppliers can rectify this without government help, particularly more rigorous provisions to ensure specification of domestic products in investment projects. A typical example is the specification in the Majes irrigation project of PVC instead of earthenware drainpipes.
37. The external requirement is spread through the projects, and not concentrated in a few.
38. See Chapter 4.3
39. This comment is, naturally, the author's personal opinion, but is based on experience of planning systems in fourteen developing countries on four continents. See also, for example, Waterston (1966). Exceptions might be Egypt and India, which are compared with Peru as examples of 'intermediate regimes' in Chapter 7.

7

Interpreting the Political Economy of Peru

7.1 Coming to Conclusions

At this stage in the study we must attempt to come to terms with the analysis as a whole, in order to make an overall evaluation of the experience of state intervention in the Peruvian economy since 1968. This will necessarily involve some exploration of future developments in the political economy, however uncertain this may appear; indeed it is implicit in any study of the past to the extent that the choice of material and viewpoint is conditioned by present problems and their possible resolution in the future. Hopefully, the analysis will permit a better understanding of current events and provide a means of critically appraising policy options for the future, but we would be content with a reasonable degree of internal consistency and some relationship to the facts.

Two themes that are central to this study are: first, the gains from the reforms in ownership, particularly the replacing of dependent domestic capitalism, and the limitations of carrying these out within a dual production structure: and second, the gains from the use of the state as 'national entrepreneur', and the limitations of carrying this out within the existing fiscal system. The problems arising from the weakness of domestic capital[1] and reliance on the powers of an essentially 'support' state[2] are so widespread that general lessons may be drawn for other developing countries, quite apart from particular issues such as land reform or oil negotiations. Generalisation from the particular is all too tempting[3], however, so that it is also an aim of this study to enable the 'forastero' to distinguish the general from the particular in the 'modelo peruano'.

After a brief summary of the economic analysis so far, and a deliniation of the main themes that emerge from it, we shall examine some alternative political interpretations of the present regime before coming to some tentative conclusions of our own in this respect. We then turn to the 1975–78 Plan, which provides a useful presentation of the government's view of the main problems, their resolution and the future of the Peruvian economy. Finally, we shall draw our own conclusions as to the significance of the Peruvian experience since 1968.

7.2 The Peruvian Economy since 1968

In this section we shall run through a brief, and hopefully coherent summary of the main elements of the study, with the intention of setting out the salient points together and underlining the most important themes. This is, naturally, a somewhat repititious process, particularly since we have already listed these in Chapter 1, but it does seem worthwhile if the somewhat tortuous argument of the rest of this Chapter is to be clarified. Having surveyed the contents of the study, we shall address ourselves to three questions: the replacement of domestic capital by the state, the reduction of external dependency and the duality of the economy.

The Peruvian economy[4] is dominated by the 'modern' sector which runs 'horizontally' through the primary, secondary and tertiary 'vertical' sectors, gathering export production, large-scale industry and finance into a network that generates two-thirds of national income but only a third of employment. The export sector provides the main motive force within this, through the current expenditure of the surplus on manufacturing production, and as the basis of the mobilisation of investment funds through the financial system into capital formation. However, although export income, and thus the economy, has grown steadily over the past two decades, the extent of industrialisation has been limited to the substitution of consumer imports and the provision of basic industrial inputs, while the rate of capital formation declined from 1961 to 1968. Closely connected to, but separated from this modern sector is the 'traditional' sector, containing the mass of peasants (producing for the domestic food market), artisans, small traders and petty service workers. This latter sector provides some two-thirds of employment but only accounts for a third of national income, forming the base of the personal income distribution. The upper reaches of this distribution are further skewed by the concentration in the ownership of the means of production.

By 1968 the main political issue had become this concentration of the productive assets in the modern sector in the hands of a few domestic oligopoly combines (the 'oligarquia') and multinational enterprises, with close links between these two groups. This ownership pattern extended through mining, fishing and export agriculture to industry and finance. During the previous decade, foreign penetration had deepened and domestic capital had taken on an almost 'rentier' role, so that by 1968 the multinational firms controlled nearly a half of private modern sector production directly, with a greater control over key branches such as mining, and indirect control through finance and technological licensing. As a result, there was little interest in 'developing' the economy as such[5], but rather a process of export-dominated growth and profit expatriation, relying on domestic savings for the investment needs of foreign corporations and linking industrial production closely to imported inputs. The same concentration of capitalist ownership also lead to neglect of the traditional economy (with implications for both income distribution and regional imbalance) on the one hand, and a narrowness in domestic markets on the other – quite apart from the threat to economic sovreignty that brought about the military intervention of 1968.

Four main areas of ownership reform have emerged[6], therefore, since that date. First, the agrarian reform, which has transformed private ownership of large agro-enterprise to workers' cooperatives; second, the exclusion of much of the foreign enterprise established in agriculture, mining, basic industry and finance; third, the extension of state enterprise by expropriation and new ventures, particularly in minerals; and lastly the introduction of worker participation in industrial management. The result of these reforms has been to reduce the degree of control over the means of production exercised by foreign and domestic capital, effectively destroying the economic power of the domestic elite and increasing that of the state correspondingly. These reforms have established the basis for state control of the economy and a higher rate of accumulation, but their effect has been confined to the modern sector, leaving the traditional worker, peasant or artisan[7] unaffected and the personal income distribution much as it was before.

The economic organisation of the state[8] is based upon that established before 1968, when it was confined to a support rather than a control function. The size of government itself has been constrained, but the rapid expansion of state enterprise in general, and its unprofitability and massive capital requirements in particular, have lead to heavy internal and external borrowing. State enterprise plays a key role in the development of the production structure, particularly in copper, oil, basic industry, food marketing and capital finance – and as a whole, the state is directly responsible for nine-tenths of exports, half of imports, a third of production and half of employment in the modern sector, as well as half the capital formation. However, although the state is, directly or indirectly, responsible for the bulk of accumulation it does not itself generate more than a small fraction of the disposable surplus in the economy. In Peruvian terms, this latter term means corporate profits, and in consequence the problem is not just one of finance but also of control over domestic production.

Economic policy[9] has been mainly concerned with stabilisation during the implementation of the ownership reforms, and in this has met with considerable success, although three problem areas have emerged: the weakness of private investment, negotiations with foreign capital, and the duality of the economy. Development planning[10] is crucial to the new role of the state as national entrepreneur, and reflects both the advantages and limitations of this new function. Sectoral and project planning have been made greatly more effective, as the result not only of improved techniques but also the dominance of state enterprise in key growth sectors. The limits of this dominance, however, mean that continued private sector control of final production for the domestic market prevents effective aggretate planning, while the 'output' orientation of the state enterprises themselves had lead to a certain neglect of 'social' policy objectives such as employment and income redistribution.

There are three themes that underly our whole analysis, and which define the freedom of action open to the state, while forming the context of the arguments presented in the rest of this Chapter in relation to the nature of the regime (Section 3), the development strategy for the rest of the decade (Sections 4 and 5) and finally the analytical conclusions of the study. These themes are as follows:

i) The most striking aspect of the Peruvian political economy has been the way in which the state has taken over so completely the function of the domestic capitalist – particularly in the formation of capital, the coordination of production and relations with foreign enterprise. The result of this process has been to break the economic power (although not the income) of the elite, by transferring to the state the basis of oligopolistic control over productive and finance capital. The absorption of exports, heavy industry and finance into the public sector has lead, however, to a structural weakness in the private sector (which was already flawed by excessive external dependence), which explains the low rate of private fixed investment and the difficulty in ensuring an adequate expansion of basic consumer goods output and the intersectoral integration of the domestic production process. The 1968–74 period essentially involved the 'estatización' of the existing modern sector, but now the more difficult task of adjusting that structure to 'desarrollo hacia adentro' rather than 'afuera' is under way.

ii) The main reason for military intervention was the failure of previous governments to negotiate firmly enough with foreign capital, and the chief aspects of this process since that date have been the nationalisation of existing foreign enterprises, the oil and copper ventures and increased public borrowing abroad. To judge whether this has reduced external dependence, four points[11] must be taken into account: (a) ownership of the means of production, (b) export of the surplus, (c) control over technology and (d) control over external finance. Both (a)[12] and (b)[13] have clearly been reduced, and will continue to be contained (despite the oil and copper concessions), particularly since private direct investment has been virtually halted. The extent of reduction in (c) is less clear, as many of the new joint state ventures are essentially means of purchasing foreign technology, but the government intends to learn through these joint ventures[14] and closely monitors other transfers[15]. The one point where external dependency has increased is (d), where the mounting burden of external private debt[16] and the financing of the next Plan[17] may well represent a real loss of autonomy.

iii) The duality of the economy[18] has been constantly mentioned in this study as placing a limit on state intervention – particularly the ownership reforms and economic policy options. This duality is expressed fundamentally by the distinction between large capitalist or state enterprises and government on the one hand and small household production units on the other, and in effect the changes in the political economy since 1968 have been concerned with the former. The consequence is to maintain the personal income distribution, narrow domestic markets[19], regional disequilibrium, stagnating food supply and internal migration. However, it is difficult to see how this could be overcome in the short or medium term, and the concentration of public investment in the modern sector, which was necessary if autonomous growth was to be attained, has meant that these contradictions in the economy and the social inequity involved remain unresolved as yet. The government is well aware of these problems, but the 'choice of technique' tends to reinforce the division, which also has a political dimension. The dominance of the modern sector is bound up with the interests of the middle class, and a determined attack on duality might well require a politically infeasible degree of resource reallocation.

These problems should not be allowed, however, to disguise the substantial progress made by the Gobierno Revolucionario de la Fuerza Armada in land reform, the reorganization of the productive system, the reduction of external dependency, the acceleration of export-led growth and the start on genuine industrialisation. In the context of a poor Latinamerican economy, these are considerable achievements.

7.3 The Nature of the Present Regime

It may rightly be considered foolhardy to attempt a 'political labelling' of any regime, particularly the Peruvian, but such an exercise in definition is essential – not for its own sake, but rather in order to put the economic analysis of this study into proper perspective. Avoidance of this task can lead to a naive belief in the economic omnipotence of the state, and thus to the attribution of any asserted shortcomings to 'inefficiency' rather than to divergence between the objectives of the state and those of the observer and to a similar disregard of the very real constraints on the freedom of action of a government imposed by the nature of its political support. Here we shall examine three alternative interpretations of the present situation, and then our own – plus a parallel. The conflicting opinions held by different authors on this subject should be seen in the light of two groups of facts: on the one hand, that the state intervention in the economy has significantly reduced external dependency and effectively replaced the domestic bourgeoisie; and on the other, the reforms have benefitted only a quarter of the population and popular mobilisation has not occurred. This contrast allows several interpretations, which stress different aspects[20] of this dichotomy, but none of these are entirely satisfactory.

The official title of the regime contains the word 'revolutionary', and several writers[21] support this interpretation, but it is difficult to see how the events in Peru since 1968 can be termed a 'revolution' in either a socialist sense[22] or in that of an 'industrial revolution' – at least, not yet. Apart from the political implications of authoritarian rule (which, after all, is the prorogative of neither right nor left), the changes in the relations of production have been mainly confined to 'horizontal' shifts in ownership rather than the 'vertical' position of labour, although the agrarian cooperatives are an exception, and the industrial communities and social property do provide potential for the future. Certainly there has been no radical income redistribution or mass mobilisation – so perhaps Hobsbawm's qualified definition as a 'peculiar revolution'[23] is more appropriate. Even so, a label such as this or that of 'revolution from above', even if deserved, does not advance the analysis very much.

The reaction of many 'radical' writers[24] is to argue that the military intervention was intended to maintain the hegemony of foreign and domestic capital, challenged by rising popular pressure during the nineteen-sixties[25]. This view was apparently consistent with the facts in the 1968–70 period, when the result of the land reform was unclear and the government was trying to stimulate private investment, but it is now untenable for a number of reasons. Among these are the evident reduction in external dependency and the expansion of state activity into economic control rather than infrastructural support, but above all the failure of the domestic bourgeoisie to re-emerge as a force in politics. This interpretation might, moreover be labelled itself as 'vulgar-marxist', and although it may well be valid elsewhere in Latin America and indeed as a description of past military interventions in Peru, it is untenable now in this original form.

In response to considerations such as these, an extension of this approach is to argue[26] that the state is engaged in the *creation* (or perhaps *re*-creation) of a true capitalist class, drawing parallels with Japan and Germany at the end of the last century. The evidence for this is based on the initial attempts to stimulate private investment, especially the compensation conditions for the land reform[27] and the 1970 industrial law, but it suffers from the same defect as the previous argument –

inconsistency with subsequent events. It may well be that this was part of original government policy,[28] but there is no positive evidence for this, and it is certainly not part of strategy now.[29] The original source for this type of analysis of 'state-led escape from backwardness' is Gerschenkron[30], and although the Russian parallel is in no sense valid either, the use of a form of state capitalism in order to accelerate industrialisation certainly is – although not as a means of fostering capitalism as such.

Having reviewed so critically the arguments of others, we must now present our own 'label'. It would seem that the outline of a typology of the 'intermediate regime' sketched by Kalecki in 1967[31] is apposite precisely because it combines apparently inconsistent features that occur in the Peruvian case in a coherent framework. He points out that a reformist government with middle-class support (such as that of Belaunde),

> " . . . to keep power . . . must:
> a) achieve not only political but also economic emancipation, i.e. to gain a measure of independence from foreign capital;
> b) carry out a land reform;
> c) assure continuous growth – this last is closely connected with the other two." (1972b, p.162).

But he also reminds us that this usually leads to conflicts with domestic and foriegn capital, and

> " . . . the final repetition of a well-known historical pattern – the final submission of the lower-middle-class to the interests of big business". (op.cit. p.163).

However, this does not apply to the Peruvian case, and Kalecki himself points out, there is another historical pattern, that of the intermediate regime,

> " . . . presented by the weakness of the native upper class and its inability to perform the role of dynamic entrepreneurs on a large scale. The basic investment for economic development must therefore be carried out by the state which lends direction to the pattern of amalgamation of the interests of the lower-middle-class with state capitalism". (op.cit. p.163).

This analysis seems to fit the Peruvian experience very well, and Kalecki goes on to argue that this 'amalgamation' is likely to be stable once installed[32], and the involvement of the military is a further stabilising factor in the Peruvian case.

Parallels with other countries are inevitably both dubious and dangerous but the similarity of the Peruvian experience in the 1969–74 period and that of Egypt in the 1956–61 period is such as to bear further examination. This latter period in Egypt[33] was one where the reformist military government implemented a radical land reform which, while dispossessing the large landowners, did not benefit the small and landless peasants. Major basic production sectors, finance and exports were nationalised, but only a minority of the workforce gained any benefits from this attack on foreign and domestic capital (i.e. those employed in the capitalist sector), while the state lacked control over final production. In consequence, so as to guarantee fulfillment of the objectives of economic strategy it was felt necessary to take over the rest of the modern sector in 1961, a move which met with little resistence from the remnants of the Egyptian bourgeoisie. As O'Brien (1966, p.240) puts it, in oddly familiar terms:

"Exhortations, incentives and indirect controls would not and could not ensure that the private sector complied with the patterns of production and investment established for it by the planners. In every case which entailed an incompatibility between ends and means the government almost invariably reacted by increasing the power of the state rather than adopting the alternative path of negotiation and compromise. Hardly ever was the Military Junta diverted from its chosen ends by the presence of traditional patterns of ownership and control over productive resources. As soon as contradictions emerged, the Junta simply altered the institutional and legal framework in order to make the economy amenable to control from the centre."

This Egyptian 'transition to socialism' became explicit after 1961, but it eventually turned out to mean dominance of the state by a bureaucratic middle class in conflict with the aspirations of the mass of the populace[34]. Although the events of 1967 make further pursuit of the parallel impossible, three aspects of the Egyptian experience – the constraints placed on reforms by the duality of the economy, the resolution of contradictions by extending state power and the dominance of the middle class – seem significant for Peru.

7.4 The 1975–78 Development Plan

The attitude of the government to the development problems we have outlined is best illustrated by the 1975–78 Development Plan, which contains the essential elements of strategy for the rest of the decade. The objectives of the Plan are framed within those for long-term development as a whole[35], but are mainly concerned with the implementation of the key oil and copper export projects, the establishment of a sound industrial base, and the rationalization of the state enterprise sector. There has been little or no consultation with the private sector over the contents of the Plan[36], which is to be mainly carried out by the public sector (with foreign cooperation in mining), and although the production of 'basic consumer goods' is mentioned as being of central importance, there are no supply programmes for these branches, which are still in private hands.

Before turning to the quantitive elements of the Plan, we should examine some aspects of the organisational basis of production proposed by the government. The main elements of the pattern of ownership are apparently intended to develop eventually into a 'core' of state enterprise, surrounded by various forms of cooperatives in the modern sector, the connection of the traditional small-scale sector remaining unclear.

"In relation to the pluralist organization of the economy, four coexistent property sectors have been defined: the social property sector, which will have most importance and priority; the state sector; the reformed sector[37]; and the small-enterprise sector, made up of the small-scale artisan, commercial and service activity. Within this system a close link will be forged . . . between the social property and state sectors, so that these constitute efficient instruments of development planning" (PRP, 1974).

The maldistribution of income within the modern sector is to be tackled by reduction of salary differentials, and positive incentives for employment in the regions, but the reduction of duality does not feature as a strategic element.

The dominant role of the state in the economy is to be maintained, and the problem of securing adequate finance is considered serious.

> "The leadership role of the state in the economic guidance of the nation will be secured by the proper finance of the public sector, so as to allow it to carry out the tasks and functions that development and national security demand . . .
> National savings will be promoted and, in particular, the savings by the central government will be increased, as will that of the state enterprises, in relation to the structures of consumption and production which the Plan postulates . . .
> The evolution of the state enterprises will be planned so as to set the period for profit generation. The state enterprises as a whole should create the basis for self-finance, establishing a compensating mechanism that allows for transfers from those with profits to those with losses" (PRP, 1974).

These measures are to be complemented by a growing share of taxation in national income, cooperatives are to be taxed as corporations, projects with a quick return are to be given priority, subsidies to be cut back unless socially necessary, and austerity in current government expenditure maintained. No radical expansion in state control over the surplus is proposed, however, although revenue should increase substantially when the export projects become operational towards the end of the decade.

The aggregate output projections[38] are remarkably realistic, forecasting an overall Gross Domestic Output growthrate (8%) somewhat above that of the previous cuatrennium (6%), but firmly based on the expected expansion of exports in 1977. The projections for sectors directly affected by state action (such as fishing, mining and construction) can be assured with some confidence, and the growth rates for agriculture and industry seem reasonably cautious. The 'non-material production' sector, however, is unlikely to be contained, given continued internal migration and the difficulty of restraining the size of government[39].

On external account, exports will remain predominantly primary, the oil and copper projects assuring the rapid expansion of the total. Imports are planned to expand at only 5% per annum (compared to 14% for exports), which seems optimistic, and might be more realistically expected to grow at 10%.

Total gross capital formation is planned to rise from 17% of GDP in 1974 to 19% in 1978, within which the public sector rate is to go up from 8.4% to 10.0%. Of this public investment schedule, there are a number of important points to be made. First, that the public share is to be over half the total during the period (two-thirds if housing is excluded) concentrating upon export projects and heavy industry. About a third of the programme is expenditure already committed to existing projects, and the remainder to new ones. By sector, the major projects are as follows: agriculture – major coastal irrigation works; industry – steel, diesel motors, machine tools[40] and shipbuilding; mining – copper and zinc refineries, Cerro Verde, Amazonian oil and the trans-Andean pipeline; and transport – roads, mostly in the central region.

On the financing side, however, the Plan is not clear at all, although it is this topic of resource acquisition (as opposed to disposition) that we have underlined as

Table 53. Aggregate Output Forecasts: 1975–78

Sector	Share of GDP (%) 1974	Share of GDP (%) 1978	Growth Rate 1974–78 (% p.a.)
Agriculture	12.6	11.0	3.3
Fishing	1.4	1.3	12.1
Mining & Oil	7.2	9.4	28.8
Industry*	28.4	29.5	8.8
Construction	5.1	6.2	13.0
Total Mat.Prodn.	54.9	57.4	8.9
Non-mat.Prodn.	45.1	42.6	6.2
Total GDP	100.0	100.0	7.7

Source: INP (1975b)
*Manufacturing and utilities

Table 54. External Trade Forecasts 1975–78 (bn soles, 1970 prices)

Exports (fob):	1974	1978	External Trade	1974	1978
Agroproducts	5.8	5.8	Exports (fob)	35.8	64.6
Fish Prods.	4.7	8.3	Exp.Services	8.4	10.2
Minerals	19.3	34.8		44.2	74.8
Oil	0.4	6.8			
Other	5.6	9.0	Imports of goods & serv.	56.9	69.1
Total	35.8	64.6			

Source: INP (1975b)

Table 55. Accumulated Investment Projections: 1975–78
(soles bn, 1973 prices)

	Public Sector	Private Sector	Total GFCF
Agriculture	31	22	53
Industry	75	57	132
Mining & Oil	98	57	155
Transport	33	16	49
Housing	5	60	65
Other	44	12	56
Total	286	224	510

Source: INP (1975b)

crucial to the development of the political economy. In round terms, assuming a balance on general government account (itself a considerable achievement), the state will have to acquire some 10% of GDP for capital formation, nearly double its net borrowing over the 1970–74 period. About half of this is apparently to be covered through the commitment by Peru's foreign creditors to finance their own exports of capital goods for the Plan[41], but this is only equivalent to a rolling forward of the public external debt to the end of the decade, thus providing a 'breathing space' until exports rise.[42] In consequence, a further 5% or more of GDP must be raised in the form of current income, either from higher tax pressure[43] or from expanded enterprise profits[44] as the internal borrowing capacity appears to have reached its limits. These are problems still to be faced.

Overall, the 1975–78 Plan does throw interesting light both on the medium-term development of the economy and on the role of the state within this. On the positive side, there is the singleminded determination to get the export projects under way while maintaining national control over national resources, and to establish the base for a genuine industrialisation process. The state control over the key sectors means that these targets can be assured, if not guaranteed, and realistic aggregate growth rates have been planned. In this context, the proposed production organization of the modern sector on the basis of the state enterprise 'core' and the surrounding cooperatives, financed from state banks and coordinated through the central planning system, has considerable potential for the future.

The weakest aspect of the Plan, and thus in the government strategy as a whole, stems from the continuing strengthening of duality. In particular, the relative neglect of food agriculture[45] and the concentration on capital-intensive projects in the public sector means that professed aims such as employment, income distribution and regional equilibrium are that much more difficult to attain. Apart from this, the lack of direct control over final domestic production pattern, and the apparent difficulty of indirect control through capital finance, mean that the composition of domestic supply is still unplanned and there is no indication that it will adjust to the needs of the mass of the population, even if it were to have the necessary income redistributed towards it. Lastly, the pricing strategy (fundamentally one of restraint – especially in food and public goods) is not consistent with the production and financing strategies outlined above.

However, it can be argued[46] that there will be plenty of time for 'social' objectives once the main elements of the new production structure have been established – and indeed this is sometimes presented as an optimal development strategy generally[47]. Against this, it can be pointed out that the political constraints on the government are such that the determination to actually carry out the resource allocation at the end of the decade may well be more difficult than it seems now. Nonetheless, the Plan does represent a realistic programme for export-led industrial development that is both planned and autonomous, a programme that may well be based on the only feasible strategy, which makes it an example to the rest of South America.

7.5 Future Economic Strategy

In a sense, the analysis of the previous section has judged the present economic strategy on its own terms, and if the concluding remarks of that section are to have substantive meaning, the strategy must be compared to some alternative. It is the intention of this section to outline such an alternative for analytical purposes, although it is argued that this does not form a viable strategy, given the existing structure of production in Peru.

Such an 'alternative strategy' would presumably consist[48] in the massive transfer of resources from the modern to the traditional sector. Arguing in arithmetic terms, as Webb (1972b) does, it would seem that if a quarter of the population receives three-quarters of personal income[49], then a one-third decrease in their incomes would double that of the other three-quarters of the population, this sum being equivalent to merely four years' growth in the standard of living of that top quartile. However, this transfer must represent real resources, either the raising of traditional sector output or the transfer of products of the modern sector, for otherwise a transfer of monetary income alone might be effectively counterbalanced by inflation in wagegoods prices. The issue, then, is not just one of arithmetic but also the generation of real income (demand) and the adjustment of the pattern of production (supply) to reach a new equilibrium.

The first step in such a transformation would be to raise income and output in peasant agriculture, mainly through higher food prices and raising land productivity. This would have three consequences: the expansion of national food supply, the increase in the incomes of the poor and the deceleration (or even reversal) of internal migration. It is not clear to what extend land productivity in the Sierra could be improved, certainly there do not appear to be significant scale economies to be gained from land consolidation[50], but much could be done with fertilisers, small machinery, storage facilities and services cooperatives within the traditional forms of peasant organization. Higher land productivity could lead either to higher incomes or more labour absorption, but to make much impact on these would require at least a doubling of output, which in turn would require a massive increase in, and reorientation of the state investment budget for agriculture. Moreover, the increase in food prices required to significantly alter the internal terms of trade would imply a corresponding reduction in real urban incomes. The use of irrigated coastal export estates for foodcrop production is another possibility, on the grounds that even though it is economically more efficient to export, say, sugar and import wheat, the employment generated would justify the change – although the absorptive potential cannot be great. On the industrial side, it would be necessary to shift towards labour-intensive manufacturing and construction, possibly on a small scale, absorbing a larger proportion of the urban labour force and producing basic mass consumption goods. This industry would be established on a regional basis and integrated to agricultural production, and wage levels in metropolitan areas held down to discourage migration, counterbalancing the spatial disequilibrium in the economy at the same time as the concentration in personal income distribution. This is a powerful argument, and presents an apparently highly desirable 'scenario', with considerable social benefits as well as the economic advantages of a wider domestic market and an integrated production structure.

Three steps in this direction are contained in the Peruvian government's programme. These are: first, the large coastal irrigation schemes[51] to stimulate food production and provide more land; second, the creation of PIARs[52] which will integrategrate the large estates, peasant producers, small industries and local services;

and third, the establishment of Propiedad Social as a means of rapidly expanding modern-sector employment[53]. However, overall economic policy, as we have seen, has not been geared to the sort of shift implied in the previous paragraph, and these three developments have not been given the budgetary or administrative support necessary to make a real impact on the problem. In crude terms, the doubling of the income of the traditional-sector worker, which would bring him up to the national mean at present, would require that roughly two-thirds of current output be invested[54] – equivalent to the accumulated public investment budget for some seven years.

But the problem is much more complex than this, as it concerns the structure of production itself. The present production system that underlies the duality of income distribution is also geared to supply the demand pattern generated by that distribution. Moreover, the natural resource endowment of Peru imposes certain characteristics on the economy, as we have seen. In practical terms, the 'alternative strategy' in its extreme form would mean abandonment of the copper, oil and heavy-industrial projects (as these use the bulk of public investment resources and provide little employment) on the one hand, and the production of many luxury consumer goods (e.g. cars) on the other, reducing aggregate national income severely in the short and medium term. Within the overall foreign exchange constraint, large sections of industry would have to be shut down or re-tooled in order to adjust to the new supply pattern and diversion of resources to agriculture. Finally, the transformation would mean a severe reduction in the absolute as well as the relative income of the top quartile – professionals, administrators and much of the urban proletariat. The underlying point is that Peru is not an agrarian economy, but an extractive-urban one, and the production and employment structure has developed in such a way as to make a 'return to the soil' virtually impossible. It is difficult to see, moreover, how such a transformation could be carried out in political terms, as it could not, presumably, be implemented by a state supported by and made up of the groups which would directly suffer from such a change, and which are also in a good position to prevent the mass mobilisation that would be, in consequence, a necessary condition of its realization.

In consequence, it seems reasonable to argue that the Peruvian economic strategy, despite its shortcomings, is the only realistic one. It consists in the rapid expansion of the modern sector based on primary exports and heavy industry, and duality is to be eventually reduced by modern employment growing more rapidly than population and the long-term transfer of resources towards peasant agriculture and small industries in the nineteen-eighties. It is a strategy which, if implemented wisely, will produce a larger, industrialized and more productive modern sector and lay the foundations for the capitalization of the traditional sector, particularly by developing the regional economies. Meanwhile, however, the symptoms of duality (such as internal migration and food shortages) cannot be expected to disappear by themselves. In consequence, it would be desirable if those branches providing for domestic consumption could be geared to labour-intensive production and incentives given to the creation of employment rather than the installation of equipment – perhaps through the state banking system's control over the bulk of capital finance to the private sector, or else extension of the public sector itself.

7.6 Concluding Remarks

The subject of this study has been the way in which the state can intervene in a dependent export economy in order to reduce the degree of external dependency and lay the foundations of sustained industrial growth. In this sense, Peru provides an important example to poor primary exporting countries which seek 'development' rather than the 'growth' that is generated by the expansion of output or rising raw material prices. In particular, the takeover of the traditional function of the economic elite (the organisation of production and the accumulation of capital) by the state provides a concrete example of a viable alternative to dependent capitalism which avoids the political risks of a rapid transition to socialism.

The achievement of the Gobierno Revolucionario de la Fuerza Armada are by any standards considerable, and more so by Latinamerican ones. They include a radical land reform, the reorganization of the fishing industry, the elimination of foreign control over exports, finance and heavy industry, the renegotiation of terms for further foreign investment, the creation of dynamic state enterprises, and the start of an ambitious industrialisation process. The emergence of a strong state from a previously weak and disarticulated public sector, expanding into the private sector and acquiring major coordination and production functions is also a substantial achievement. It is impossibly to argue that the transformation thus effected by anything but a substantial step forward in the economic development of Peru.

However, there have appeared a series of severe limitations on the ownership reforms and the 'depth' of economic development. These arise from the dual nature of the structure of production, which limited the coverage of the capitalist sector to one-third of the workforce, and thus both the scope of the ownership reforms and the proportion of the population benefited. The bulk of the peasants, artisans and tertiary workers are excluded, but it is difficult to see how this could have been avoided in the short or medium term. The other limitation of the reforms is that they do not confer state control over final production for the domestic market, making production planning difficult to implement. The main functional weakness of state intervention, however, is the narrow resource base of the public sector, which means that the state must borrow on a restricted domestic capital market and increasingly abroad to finance the massive burden of accumulation it has undertaken.

Despite these limitations, and without underplaying the shortcomings of Peruvian development policy in areas such as employment and regionalisation, it would appear that the strategy outlined in the 1975–78 Plan is the best option open to the government. The large oil and copper projects are to be commissioned as rapidly as possible, and an industrial base built up around the creation of a capital goods sector and expansion in steel and chemicals. However, the attainment of the Plan and the financial problems of the state may well lead logically to either further absorption of the means of production into the state sector or serious dependence upon external official finance – and both of these would imply considerable political change. Thus, although the main lines of economic development for the rest of the decade are now reasonably clear, the political equilibrium itself must move either right or left.

The Peruvian experience since 1968 represents, then, an interesting example of state intervention in a dependent export economy so as to reduce that dependency and assure autonomous economic development. It may well set an important precedent for Latin America and possibly for the underdeveloped world as a whole.

NOTES TO CHAPTER 7

1. See Baran (1957)
2. See Griffin & Enos (1972)
3. Particularly about Latin America, given its apparent socio-economic homogeneity.
4. See Chapter 2.
5. There is no normative condemnation in this statement – capitalists are out to make profits and if in particular circumstances the only way to do this is in industry, then they will industrialise. If, however, maximum return is to be gained from commerce or finance, then this is what they will do, and it is illogical to expect otherwise.
6. See Chapter 3.
7. And those only peripherally attached to the modern sector, such as seasonal labour on the estates.
8. See Chapter 4.
9. See Chapter 5.
10. See Chapter 6.
11. See Chapter 2.1
12. See Chapter 3.2
13. See Chapter 5.3
14. See Chapter 4.3
15. See Chapter 5.3
16. Idem
17. See Section 4 of this Chapter.
18. See Chapter 2.1
19. In spite of the reforms, the domestic market for manufactures is still effectively confined to a third of the population, which accounts for as much as seven-tenths of personal income and a greater share of the demand for industrial products. The key point, however, is that this distorted income distribution leads to a demand for highly differentiated products that are intensive in both capital and technology, at the expense of simple manufactures (i.e. wagegoods) produced by 'simple' industry expanding into a dynamic internal market. Unfortunately, it is not possible to measure the 'width' of domestic markets statistically, because the distinction is one of 'quality' rather than 'type' of product, a difference that does not turn up in budget surveys.
20. In this context the different viewpoints of economists and sociologists, who would logically stress the former and latter aspects respectively, is worth noting.
21. See Delgado (1972), and numerous official sources.
22. Indeed, the official definition is 'ni capitalista ni comunista' – see Zimmerman (1974)
23. In the New York Review of Books. 16.12.75.
24. Such as Quijano (op.cit.) upon whom most other writers on the left appear to base their analysis. Quijano himself appears to have moved towards the position expressed in the next paragraph, but it is curious to note that his original view that the government was fundamentally at one with foreign business is eagerly quoted by authors as distinct from him as Ingram (1974) and Goodsell (1974).
25. An alternative form of this argument is that the reforms are merely intended to 'head off communism', but there is no evidence that this was really imminent, especially after the rural guerrillas were crushed in 1966.
26. See Petras & LaPorte (1971), Wils (1975).
27. Particularly the use of agrarian reform bonds as collateral for industrial finance from

state banks, but in fact this facility (of which so much was made by critics) has not been used to any extent – see Chapter 3.3

28. It *is* clear that the government took some time to realize what a mortal blow the reform had dealt to domestic capitalism.
29. See the next Section of this Chapter.
30. Gerschenkron (1966), analysing tzarist policy at the turn of the century.
31. Kalecki (1972b). He does not, naturally, discuss Peru.
32. Kalecki asserts that this combination, although internally stable, might succumb to "external pressures . . . from the imperialist powers and big business", but in the Peruvian case, such pressure appears to have lead to more radicalisation in the military regime rather than less.
33. See O'Brien (1966).
34. See Mabro (1974).
35. For the National Objectives, see Chapter 1.3. The qualitative elements are given in the 'Limanientos del Plan Nacional de Desarrollo 1975–78' (PRP, 1974).
36. See Chapter 6.2
37. Author's note – this means the private firms in the modern sector with worker participation, which should have reached about a quarter share in the equity by the end of the decade – see Chapter 3.5
38. INP (1975b) and working drafts. See also the discussion in *The Andean Report* Vol.1.2, (Lima, July 1975).
39. Planned to fall from an estimated 8% of GDP in 1974 to 7% in 1978.
40. The 'metalmecanica' programme under the Andean Pact.
41. The 'Consultative Group' is made up of Peru's main creditors (USA, Canada, Japan, Spain and the EEC), chaired by the IBRD. It met in Paris during April 1975 – see *Lat.Amer.Econ.Rep.*, Vol.II.7 (London 2.5.75).
42. The object of the creditors, according to *L.A.E.R.* (op.cit.), was to ensure metropolitan control over the mineral and oil supplies.
43. See Chapter 4.2
44. See Chapter 4.3
45. The coastal irrigation projects may well ameliorate the urban food supply position, but not highland peasant poverty.
46. And this is, indeed, the position of the INP.
47. See the discussion in Griffin & Enos (1972)
48. There is another alternative, that of returning to 'dependent capitalism', which we do not consider. Unfortunately, the 'radical critics' of the government (e.g. Quijano, 1971), who implicitly propose a transformation such as that discussed here, do not specify how it might be achieved.
49. See Chapter 2.4
50. Horton (1974)
51. Projects under way should eventually create some 0.57 million hectares of irrigated coastal land (compared to 0.75 at present), absorbing some 0.1 million families – a considerable achievement, but benefitting a relatively small proportion of the total peasantry.
52. See Chapter 3.3, and also Horton (1974).
53. See Chapter 3.5
54. Based on a rough capital-output ratio of 2.

Appendix I

The Intersectoral Structure of the Economy

It has been argued both that the Peruvian economy is 'disarticulated' in the sense of insufficient intersectoral integration (e.g. Baulne, 1974), and that the economy is overly geared towards export requirements (e.g. Saberbein, 1973). These two propositions appear somewhat contradictory, but to some extent the problem should be susceptible to quantitative resolution. In order to answer a number of questions about the productive structure of the Peruvian economy, and throw light upon the problem mentioned above, a brief analysis of the 1969 Input-Output Table is presented in this Appendix. The main computational procedure involved is the 'collapse' of the original 40-sector table into five sectors, allowing the underlying structure of the economy to be seen more clearly – these five relating to the functional operations of the economy rather than the conventional classification. The specific questions to be tackled relate to the degree of integration between these major sectors and their overall 'import-intensity'. Ideally, such an analysis should be carried out so as to cover a reasonable time-period (say 1959 as well as 1969) but there exist no estimates on a comparable basis for use in such an exercise, and indeed, it appears that no analysis of the Input-Output Table along these lines has been carried out as yet.

The first stage in the computation is to aggregate the 1969 Input-Output Table (INP, 1973c), collapsing the original forty sectors into five: 'Exports', 'Food Agriculture', 'Final Material Production for the Domestic Market (FMP)', 'Intermediate Material Production (IMP)' and 'Service' sectors. These new sectors are mainly self explanatory, apart from the regrouping of the 'export' sector so as to include primary and secondary sectors concerned in the export process, and the inclusion of construction under 'FMP'. These definitions reflect the real divisions in the economy, and avoid, say, the artificial division of cane production from sugar refining that occurs in the national accounts.

In the process of aggregation, the unit of measurement has been increased from soles 10^3 to soles 10^8, both for convenience and also because even the latter degree of significance may be more than the original data can bear (i.e. one part in a thousand in the totals). There are also certain inconsistencies in the INP table as it stands, which in this Note have been absorbed into the 'Service' sector.

Table A–1 shows the result of these computations, and is directly comparable with the original. It shows the inter-sectoral purchases, imported inputs (competitive and non-competitive), value added and total sales (the rows) and intersectoral sales, consumption, exports and total sales (the columns). All values are at producer

Table A–1. Aggregated Input-Output Matrix for 1969 (Units: 100 thousand soles)

	Exp.	Agric.	FMP	IMP	Serv.	Intermed. Demand.	Domest. Consum.	Exports	Gross Sales
Export Prodn.	162	0	33	35	0	230	35	283	548
Agric.	0	65	40	3	0	108	214	4	326
Fin.Mat.Prod.	7	21	101	7	38	174	482	39	695
Int.Mat.Prod.	30	6	68	44	62	210	186	9	405
Services	39	1	55	32	184	311	795	0	1106
Tot.Dom.Inputs	238	93	297	121	284	1033			
Compet.Imports	30	3	63	43	20				
Non-Comp.Imports	5	2	25	53	0				
Total Inputs	273	98	385	217	304				
Value Added	275	228	310	188	802				
Gross Sales	548	326	695	405	1106				3080

prices. Table A–2 shows the result of eliminating intra-sectoral transactions so as to give only the flows between the aggregate sectors defined. Finally, Table A–3 shows some relevant indices of 'integration' for the sectors, which will be discussed below; they are drawn directly from Table 2.

From these tables, the following general points may be derived:

a) The degree of integration of the 'export' sector can be seen directly from Tables A–2 and A–3. The export sector is clearly a dominant one in the economy (27% of value added in material production) and has a high ratio of direct value-added in total sales (71%). But 32% of its inputs from other sectors are imported and indirect imports (i.e. required to produce domestic inputs) raise this figure to 40%. The sector does not provide inputs to other sectors to any great extent, as would be expected, and only takes 5% of industrial output. Thus, although the sector cannot be defined as an 'enclave', its effect on the domestic economy (apart from its statistical contribution to GDP) is more through the expenditure of income (i.e. value added) as wages, tax and profits, than through the linkage effects.

b) The outstanding feature of the 'industrial' (FMP and IMP) sectors is their degree of import-dependence (see Table A–3), meaning that the final industrial outputs import nearly a third of their inputs, and intermediate industry over a half; making manufactured goods have a total import content of some 20%. The relatively low proportion of intersectoral sales by IMP may be surprising, but much of the 'capital goods' output is really producing consumer durables, such as washing machines. The low proportion of exports in sales (only 5% for IMP and FMP) should also be noted. These figures throw some light upon the import-substitution process of the 1960's, which almost eliminated consumer goods imports (apart from food) but still requires considerable amounts of imported inputs. Moreover, the relatively high level of 'competitive' (i.e. capable of domestic supply if capacity were expanded) imports should be noted, making a total of 65% of all imports.

c) As far as the productive structure as a whole is concerned, Table A–3 shows the low degree of sectoral integration (indicated by intersectoral over total sales) and thus the high degree of 'verticality' – that is, the high proportion of imports and value-added directly involved in production. Clearly this measure is a relative matter, and comparison would be necessary with other economies (e.g. Colombia), but the disarticulation is striking. It can be, and is argued that principles of efficient resource usage, comparing imports and domestic production for minimum cost, mean that an efficient production structure is not necessarily an integrated one (e.g. Little & Mirrlees, 1968). Nonetheless, it is difficult to see how, in the long run, true industrialization (as opposed to import-substitution) can be achieved without greater integration in general, and the development of a capital-goods sector in particular. Moreover, the structure of industry also reflects the patterns of demand and ownership, both of which have, in the past, been such as to promote excessive external dependence. Important intersectoral linkages do exist, but in the form of ownership groups, which are concerned not only with input-output relationship but with the

Table A–2. Aggregate Input-Output Matrix – Intersectoral Flows Only

	Exp.	Agric.	FMP	IMP	Serv.	Intermed. Demand.	Domest. Consum.	Exports	Gross Sales
Export Prodn.	–	0	33	35	0	68	35	283	386
Agric.	0	–	40	3	0	43	214	4	261
FMP	7	21	–	7	38	73	482	39	594
IMP	30	6	68	–	62	166	186	9	361
Services	39	1	55	32	–	127	795	0	922
Dom.Inp.	76	28	196	77	100	477	1712	335	
Import	35	5	88	96	20	244			
V.Added	275	228	310	188	802	1803			
Net Sales	386	261	594	361	922				2523

Table A–3. Indices of Integration

	Exports(A)	Agric(B)	FMP(C)	IMP(D)	Serv.(E)
Intersectoral/Total Sales	17%	16%	12%	46%	14%
Imported/Total Inputs	32%	16%	31%	55%	2%
Total Inputs/Sales	29%	13%	48%	48%	13%
Exports/Sales	73%	2%	7%	2%	. .

shifting of surpluses from saving in one enterprise to investment in another, as was seen in Chapter 2.6.

d) The inversion of the production coefficients matrix enables the final input requirements of any production sector to be determined, showing the final value-added and import proportions for each sector.

Table A–4. Final Input Requirements

	Value Added	Imports
Export Sector	88%	12%
Food Ag.	96%	4%
Final Mat. Prodtn.	82%	18%
Intmd. Mat. Prodtn.	71%	29%
Service Sector	95%	5%

e) The aggregation of the table involves a certain loss of detail (although the apparent accuracy of the original is deceptive), which has been useful for our purposes in this Appendix. Nonetheless, further exploration of the full table would be useful, particularly in order to identify those particular industries which represent the least integration and most imported inputs, and are thus the greatest strain on the balance of payments, for closer investigation.

The classification of the five sectors is given below, accompanied by the original column/row numbers in the INP Table. The criteria are to a certain extent arbitrary (e.g. 'industrial crops', such as cotton, go to domestic industry as well as export) but are valid for the broad analysis of this Appendix.

A: Export Sector
1. Industrial Crops
6. Fishing
7. Mining (extraction of minerals)
8. Petroleum extraction
9. Fishmeal Processing
11. Sugar Refining
27. Non-ferrous Metals.

B: Domestic Agriculture
2. Food Crops
3. Forestry
4. Cattle-raising
5. Dairy Products.

C: Final Domestic Material Production
10. Food Industry
12. Drinks

13.	Tobacco	18.	Furniture
14.	Textiles	19.	Paper
15.	Shoes	20.	Printing
16.	Clothing	32.	Misc. Manufacturing
17.	Wood Products	33.	Construction.

D: Intermediate Domestic Material Production

21.	Leather	28.	Metal Products
22.	Rubber	29.	Non-electrical machinery
23.	Chemicals	30.	Electrical machinery
24.	Gasoline etc.	31.	Transport Equipment
25.	Non-metallic minerals	34.	Energy.
26.	Iron and Steel		

E: Service Sector

35.	Commerce	38.	Education and Health
36.	Banks etc.	39.	Housing
37.	Transport	40.	Other Services.

The Input-Output Table compiled by the INP does not appear to have been explicitly reconciled to the National Accounts, compiled by the Central Bank (BCR, 1974a). At an aggregate level, the sum of value added (180 billion soles) and the excess of exports over imports (10) given in the Table yields an implicit GDP estimate (190) somewhat lower than that given in the Cuentas Nacionales (209).

The inversion of the Table to produce the unit input requirements, is based on input coefficients (expressed as a proportion of gross sales):

		A	B	C	D	E
Sectors	A	–	. .	0.056	0.097	. .
	B	. .	–	0.067	0.008	. .
	C	0.018	0.080	–	0.019	0.041
	D	0.078	0.023	0.114	–	0.067
	E	0.101	0.004	0.093	0.089	–
Imports		0.091	0.019	0.148	0.266	0.022
Value Added		0.712	0.874	0.522	0.521	0.870

This is the 'A' matrix, the inverse being the $(I-A)^{-1}$ matrix:

	1	2	3	4	5
1	1.010	0.009	0.068	0.100	0.010
2	0.003	1.006	0.075	0.010	0.004
3	0.025	0.083	1.015	0.027	0.044
4	0.089	0.034	0.132	1.018	0.074
5	0.113	0.167	0.128	0.103	1.012

The final input requirements of each sector are obtained by multiplying inverse coefficients (Z_{ij}) by the relevant final input coefficient (Y_i) to give the total requirements ($\Sigma_i Z_{ij} Y_i$) for each sector (j), shown in the text.

Appendix II

Quantifying the Reforms

In this Appendix we shall explore the statistical basis of two of the key tables in the study – the estimation of the duality (Table 2) and that of the extent of the post-1968 reforms (Table 19). These estimates are approximate, to say the least, although the essential nature of the results appears to be relatively robust.

We proceed in two stages. First we estimate the distribution of net output (i.e. value-added) and employment between the 'modern' and 'traditional' sectors. Second, we divide the modern sector between functional sub-sectors 'before' and 'after' the reforms. In order to standardise the analysis, and avoid having to take into account the changes in the economy itself between 1968 and 1974, the output and employment structure for 1972 has been used as the basis for the calculations. The analysis for the first stage is more accurate, and based on clear definitions, but that for the second is more of an 'informed guess'. This analysis, however, would form a useful research topic for investigation in depth.

The estimate of duality can be compared with the statistically more sophisticated work in Webb (1973), and despite the 'overlap' of sectors resulting from his use of *personal* income distribution, our results are not inconsistent with his. However, our approach is based on an analytically more relevant 'functional' rather than a 'personal income' division. The estimates for the scale of reform are not known to have been attempted elsewhere, but again, Webb (1973) estimated the effect of the reforms upon personal income to 1972, and we have quoted his conclusions in Chapter 3.

The criterion for the division between 'modern' and 'traditional' sectors corresponds roughly to enterprises of large and medium scale in the former, and small (i.e. less than five employees) in the latter. The source for the original sectoral framework for output and employment is BCR (1974a), and for the allocation is:

a) Agriculture – all export agriculture (Appendix I) output, and employment from MinAg (1974).
b) Mining, Fishing – all modern.
c) Industry – Manufacturing, utilities from MIT 'Estadistica Industrial' and totals from BCR (1974a).
d) Government, Banking – all modern.
e) 'Other' – commerce from 1963 Economic Census (Appendix IV), services from 1961 Population Census (Appendix IV), author's estimate for rest.

This yields the table below, expressed in thousandths of the total output or employment – an unrealistic degree of accuracy quickly abandoned in the aggregate tables.

Table A–5. Dual Structure of Output and Employment

	Output			Employment		
	Total	Modern	Tradit.	Total	Modern	Tradit.
Agriculture	169	68	101	445	115	330
Fishing	31	31	–	14	14	–
Mining	62	62	–	22	22	–
Manufacturing	190	124	66	140	47	93
Construction	47	19	28	42	21	21
Utilities	11	11	–	4	4	–
Transport	52	16	36	35	4	–
Commerce	132	100	32	109	44	65
Banking	32	32	–	7	7	–
Government	97	97	–	73	73	–
Services	177	53	124	109	11	98
Total	1000	613	387	1000	362	638

This, then gives us the allocation between modern and traditional sectors. In the table presented in the main text, the 'export' sector is made up of modern agriculture, mining and fishing, along with that part of manufacturing dedicated to export processing. Incidentally, if this analysis were to be carried out for different years, it is doubtful whether the balance of duality has altered much since 1961 – due to the shift between traditional agriculture and services. Certainly, Webb (1973) shows little change over this period.

Table A–6. Duality of the Economy

	Output	Workforce
Modern	61%	36%
Traditional	39%	64%
Total	100%	100%

The second stage consists in the allocation of production and workforce in the *modern* sector between four groups: 'state', 'foreign capital', 'domestic capital' and 'cooperatives'. The 'before' estimate corresponds to data for 1968 on the shares of each production (and employment) sector held by each functional sub-sector, based on the production and employment pattern for 1972. The 'after' estimate is based on the cumulative effects of the ownership reforms between 1968 and 1974 upon ownership, and thus on these functional sub-sectoral shares (rather than upon personal income distribution), based again on the production and employment structure for 1972. The sources are many, and correspond to those discussed in Chapter 3. The 'row' allocation for employment is pro-rata to that for output, which implies an assumption that the capital/labour ratios are equal within them.

Table A–7. The Reform Matrix

BEFORE

	Output				Employment			
	Total	State	F.Cap	D.Cap	Total	State	F.Cap	D.Cap
Agriculture	68	–	17	51	115	–	29	86
Fishing	31	–	16	15	14	–	7	7
Mining	62	–	53	9	22	–	19	3
Industry	135	4	73	58	51	1	28	22
Banking	32	8	16	8	7	2	3	2
Government	97	97	–	–	73	73	–	–
Other	188	–	29	159	80	–	12	68
Total	613	109	204	300	362	76	98	188

AFTER

	Output				Employment			
	State	F.Cap	D.Cap	Coop.	State	F.Cap	D.Cap	Coop.
Agriculture	–	–	17	51	–	–	29	86
Fishing	31	–	–	–	14	–	–	–
Mining	25	28	9	–	9	10	3	–
Industry	47	43	38	7	18	16	14	3
Banking	21	1	10	–	5	–	2	–
Government	97	–	–	–	73	–	–	–
Other	38	10	140	–	16	4	60	–
Total	259	82	214	58	135	30	108	89

Summarising from these two tables, we have table A–8

Table A–8. Summary Reform Matrix

	Before		After	
	Output	Employment	Output	Employment
State	11	7	26	13
Foreign Capital	20	10	8	3
Domestic Capital	30	19	21	11
Cooperatives	–	–	6	9
Total Mod.Sector	61	36	61	36

Appendix III

The Flow of Funds

The core of any discussion of the role of the state in the surplus mobilisation process should include a Flow-of-Funds Analysis, indicating the sources and uses of funds in the public and private sector, and how these are inter-related. In our case, we are particularly interested in the way in which savings is translated into capital formation – and as savings and investment in these two sectors are far from balanced, a considerable 'net' as well as 'gross' flow of funds must take place between them. We are attempting, therefore, to deal with only *capital* flows and to integrate these with the 'real' economy as represented by the national accounts.

A considerable study of the flow-of-funds in the Peruvian financial system has been carried out by the Ministry of Finance, resulting in the published estimates for 1965–70 (CNSEV, 1973) and current work on 1971–73. These, however, have a major shortcoming from our point of view, in that they are concerned with *all* financial flows, where current transactions such as short-term credit predominate, and thus the capital flows cannot be easily distinguished. Moreover, in practical terms, these estimates have not been reconciled either with the public sector accounts on the one hand, or with the national accounts on the other. Nonetheless, the resulting estimates of asset-holding are useful in elucidating the origins of saving in the private sector, as we have seen in Chapter 2.

The other potential source is the public sector accounts themselves, especially the capital budgets given in INP (1974b), and discussed in Chapter 4.4. The difficulty with these, however, is that they are not explicitly related to the financial sector as a whole, and moreover they contain a number of items (e.g. debt servicing) which do not correspond to 'savings' or 'investment' in 'economic' (i.e. national-accounting) terms, but they are useful when reconciled with the national accounts, as we shall see.

In consequence, in order to illustrate the process discussed in the first paragraph, it has proved necessary to construct a flow-of-funds matrix specifically related to the requirements of our analysis. The procedure is extremely simple, and essentially based on the national accounts – here we shall illustrate the calculations with the figures for 1973. The first stage is to take total fixed capital formation and savings (net of stockbuilding) figures, from BCR (1974a) and divide these between the state and private sectors by subtracting the state element, using the sources mentioned in Chapter 4. Clearly, then, a net transfer of some 23.5 billion soles must have taken place into the public sector, made up of three elements:

Table A–9. Savings and Investment (1973, soles billion)

Savings:	State	–2.0	Fixed Investment:	
	Private Domestic	47.4	Public	21.5
	Foreign (net)	4.7	Private	28.6
	Total	50.1	Total	50.1

i) net loans (i.e. loans net of amortisation) from the foreign sector to the public sector;
ii) flows from the public sector into the private (i.e. development loans etc.);
iii) flows from the private sector into the public, including not only loans but also net deficit financing.

Of these three, the first two are relatively simple to estimate, but the third is complicated by the credit operations of the central banking system and deficit finance, so that it is this item that we shall derive by deduction. The sources, then, are as follows:

i) the public external debt estimates, supplied by the BCR;
– the foreign finance for the private sector then being found from the national accounts' foreign savings less (i);
ii) the investment operations of the development banks ('banca estatal de fomento'), from BCR (1974c);
iii) the balance required to equalise the 'sources' and 'uses' totals.

We now have, therefore, table A–10.

Table A–10. The Flow of Funds Matrix:

		State	Private
Sources:	Own Savings	–2.0	47.4
	Foreign	13.3	–8.6
	Intersectoral	28.7	18.5
	Total	40.0	57.3
Uses:	Fixed Investment	21.5	28.6
	Intersectoral	18.5	28.7
	Total	40.0	57.3

The repetition of this procedure for each of the years in question gives us a set of matrices, the flows for the public sector being shown in table A–11. This table, when divided through by the GDP in that year, yields the table in Chapter 4.4.

Finally, for 1973 we show a total flow-of-capital funds matrix, table A–12, which employs the convention that the government borrows and the enterprises lend for expository simplicity, but see the discussion in Chapter 4.4.

Table A–11. Sources and Uses of State Funds: 1969–73 (soles bn)

		1969	1970	1971	1972	1973
Sources:	Own savings	4.4	4.9	1.6	2.2	–2.0
	Domestic Borrowing	2.6	11.2	21.1	21.9	28.7
	Foreign (net)	5.7	3.0	1.2	5.2	13.3
	Total	12.7	19.1	23.9	29.3	40.0
Uses:	Fixed Investment	8.8	10.9	12.8	14.8	21.5
	Domestic Lending	3.9	8.2	11.1	14.5	18.5

Table A–12. Flow of Capital Funds in 1973 (soles bn)

	State Sector			Private Sector	Total Transf.	Gross Fix. Cap.Form.	Total Uses
	Govt.	Enterp.	Total				
State:							
Govt.	–	30.5	30.5	–	30.5	8.8	39.3
Enterp.	–	–	–	18.5	18.5	12.7	31.2
Total	–	30.5	30.5	18.5	49.0	21.5	70.5
Private Sector	42.0	–	42.0	–	42.0	28.6	70.6
Total Transf.	42.0	30.5	72.5	18.5	91.0	50.1	141.1
Own Saving	–2.7	0.7	–2.0	47.4	45.4	–	45.4
Total Sources	39.3	31.2	70.5	65.9	136.4	50.1	186.5

Appendix IV

Sources of Data on the Economy

The object of this Appendix is to discuss, in greater length than is possible in footnotes, the general nature of the data sources employed for the economic analysis in this study. We shall not attempt to explore all the relevant sources on the economy presently available, let alone those for the modern economy as a whole, particularly since the forthcoming 'Economic History of Modern Peru' by Rosemary Thorp and Geoffrey Bertram (Columbia U.P., 1977) will provide a thorough survey. Rather, we shall discuss the main sources of quantitative data used in this study in relation to their scope and reliability so as to throw more light upon their use as supporting evidence for the arguments in the analysis. The qualitative sources are indicated by the Bibliography, upon which see also Matos (1971).

As a whole, the publicly available data on the Peruvian economy is poor both in quantity and quality, presumably because the demand (as opposed to the need) for reliable statistics has not existed. A consequence of this has been a series of problems in policy implementation – a crucial example being the way in which the limits of the ownership reforms (i.e. the scope of the modern sector) were not anticipated, as we have seen in Chapter 3. Only one economic census has ever been completed (1963) and that for 1973 will not be ready until 1976 at the earliest. There is a crucial lack, above all, of current indices of production on the one hand, and cross sectional studies of consumption on the other. There is no official estimate of income-distribution, Webb (1972b) being the pioneer effort in essentially a personal research project. In consequence, it is difficult for either the planners or the policymakers to diagnose current problems accurately, or to anticipate the consequence of alternative actions. This means that government activities tend to be framed in reference to the public sector itself, and to specific modern-sector activities such as mining and heavy industry, with little idea of what is needed or what might be done for, say, food agriculture.

Here we shall discuss four main groups of quantitative material, most of the relevant studies of the political economy having been quoted on relevant occasions in the body of the text. These are: the work on the national accounts and financial statistics by the Central Reserve Bank; the work on population censi and annual abstracts by the Oficina Nacional de Estadistica y Censos (ONEC); the public sector accounts prepared by the Ministry of Finance and the INP; and lastly the statistical publications. There appear to be few sources of quantitative information outside the public sector, although the socio-economic research institute of the Catholic University (CISEPA) publishes a valuable series of analytical documents in related fields (a number of which are cited in the text) which contain some of the more important pieces of 'private' quantitative research. In particular, there is no independent estimate of economic progress outside the state, the sole exception being the quarterly report of the Banco Continental (and even this is now a 'banco asociado'), apart, of course, from the press, discussed below. Conversely, the government has its own internal economic intelligence service (see Chapter 6) based on quarterly reports to the INP from the OSP in each ministry – but these are confidential documents. Outside Peru, the only official publication of importance is the short section on Peru in each ECLA 'Economic Survey' (two years after the year in question), and the unpublished IBRD annual report – and this latter, if obtainable, is indicative of the World Bank's attitude to post-1968 Peru as well as that of the state of the economy itself.

The major source of information on the economy, and also the most reliable, is the work of the Central Bank, which is charged with the compilation of the national accounts. Apart from these, the Bank also publishes (in the monthly Boletin and the annual Memoria) a very good coverage of finance (bank credit, reserves, monetary phenomena and external trade) with about a quarter's delay. The compilation of the national accounts is the major contribution to statistical information on the economy – the main sets of interest to this study being the series covering the period 1950–65 (BCR, 1967) and 1960–73 (BCR, 1974a). The notes to both these volumes explain the methodology in disarming detail, and while it is apparent that this methodology represented a pioneering effort a decade ago, it is perhaps unfortunate that little modification has been made since. There are a number of weaknesses that should be noted:

a) The investment estimates are derived by multiplying sales of capital goods (essentially imported equipment and domestic construction materials) by a fixed ratio (taken, apparently from the 1963 census) and not from sample surveys, so no sectoral figures are available. Moreover, private savings are defined as equal to this plus stockbuilding reports from the Bank's own annual survey of major enterprises, and private investment by deduction of that in the public sector;
b) The coverage of employment by sector is based on extrapolation from the 1940 and 1961 censi rather than from current surveys, which in turn is used as a basis for calculating 'output' in the service and commerce sectors;
c) The functional income distribution is based on the Bank survey estimate of profits from the major enterprises as reported by themselves and the official labour wage rates, excludes expatriated profits, and is considered unreliable;
d) There is considerable disagreement between the BCR and the Ministry of Industry over the estimate of value added in manufacturing, but most of this appears to derive from differences in the proportion of that generated in the processing of primary exports to be included.

Nonetheless, it should not be forgotten that the BCR figures are the most reliable and (importantly) the only coherent economic statistics for Peru, and this study has relied upon them extensively, particularly in the disentanglement of government accounts. In support of the national accounts the BCR also issues a number of mimeo documents from time to time including statistical series for production, external trade and financial movements, which are of considerable interest.

The ONEC is the body officially responsible for the coordination of statistical data and the execution of censi. The latter task is not one of great frequency; the 1972 population exercise being only the fourth in the history of the Republic (1876, 1940, 1961), and in 1974 preliminary results were released. These are valuable sources for occupation and migration as well as the characteristics of the population itself. The only completed economic census is that for 1963 (preceded by a rural land-use survey in 1961), released in 1967, but this covers only agriculture, manufacturing and commerce, and although mining and finance are well covered by their own sources, the exclusion of services and transport is serious – as these are two of the 'traditional' activities of which we know the least. The 1973 economic census (to be released in 1976) should have a broader coverage and depth, as well as giving a valuable insight into the results of the post-1974 reforms. There is no system of sample surveying of any kind, which means that annual estimates of population and occupation are necessarily interpolative, and the 'traditional sector' is neglected by the available statistics. Apart from this, the ONEC is responsible for the compilation of data from various sources within the public sector for the Anuario Estadistico, of which the only volumes since 1960 appear to be those for 1966 (published 1968), 1969 (1971) and 1971 (1974), which are used in this study. Unfortunately, although the responsible agency is cited for each table, the methodology is not given and the frequent discrepancies with data from these same sources cannot be reconciled. The ONEC also compiles the only cost-of-living index (for Lima-Callao), but the weights date from 1964. The ONEC itself is grossly understaffed and underequipped and does not even possess a complete collection of government publications, these being haphazardly deposited in the Archivo Nacional and allegedly uncatalogued since 1968.

Of the official sources on the economy, the ministries are generally responsible for their sectors, but these tend to confine their statistics to the 'modern' part of their domain. Of relevance to this study are the production statistics from the following ministries: Finance (banking, fiscal accounts, external trade); Industry ('Estadistica Industrial': annual production, employment, value added and investment by branch); Agriculture (annual crop estimates and 'hojas de balance', both said to be unreliable, and the 'Gaceta Verde' a magazine on land reform); Fishing (catches, processing); Energy and Mines (output, and in the case of the latter, consolidated enterprise accounts); Transport (ports, airports and vehicle registrations); Housing (construction, building permits); Labour (registered unemployed, strikes etc.); and Commerce (wholesale and retail price indices). There are two major difficulties with these sources in relation to research: the first is that they rarely indicate the methodology employed, which often varies from one year to another; and the second is that they are usually issued in limited numbers and in mimeo form, so that once the original 'edition' has run out, back numbers can be obtained only with extreme difficulty. From the rest of the public sector only the Banco Industrial used to produce an annual survey of industry, but this has not appeared since 1971. The INP itself does not publish statistical material and although a number of its studies (among which are those quoted in the text) are circulated within the public sector, the only publicly available material of significance are the Development Plans.

The main source for public sector finance is the annual edition of the Cuenta General de la Republica Peruana. These have been published since 1922 (the date of the first Ley Organica del Presupuesto, before that there has been fragmentary 'Estados') by the Controloria General, and up to 1963 cover current central government account well, but capital operations and deficit finance are treated badly, if at all. In 1963, the budgetary reform introduced a system of programme budgeting, and although the 1964 Cuenta is somewhat chaotic, the standard for 1965–67 is high, covering the rest of the public sector well. 1968 was (understandably) deficient, and the last available year is 1970 (published in 1974). The BCR, however, does disentangle the main items and present them on a consistent basis for the 1965–72 period in BCR (1974b). The INP, as we have seen, compiles analyses of the investment budgets and expenditures, while the annual budget speech of the Minister of Finance usually contains data on the current position on public sector accounts.

Turning to the private sources, some mention should be made of the usual range of company reports and publications by bodies such as the Sociedad Nacional de Industrias and the Camera de Comericio, but both the number and quality of them has declined since 1968, as might be expected. To some extent their place has been taken by the annual reports of state enterprises (e.g. PETROPERU, AEROPERU, COFIDE) but the data on the private sector is now very poor.

Finally, of course, the domestic and international press is a constant if sometimes unreliable source of current material. It is, clearly an indispensable source for political events, but the announcement of, say, major investment projects and sectoral production results tends to be ill-defined and often refer to plans rather than realities. The indispensible source for all topics where foreign capital is involved is the (weekly) *Peruvian Times* (closed early in 1975), but it is not highly reliable on the economy and domestic politics. The former, since 1968 at least, is best covered by *Oiga*, and the latter by *Caretas* (Lima, weekly and fortnightly, respectively) among the Peruvian sources – while *Latin America* and *Latin American Economic Report* (both London, weekly) are probably the best foreign sources. Major international newspapers (e.g. Le Monde, N.Y. Herald) usually cover major political events, while the financial press (Economist, Wall Street Journal etc.) cover new projects and financial deals. However, we have not used these sources in this study, for two reasons – firstly because this particular area is not well covered by the press, and second because the author's own access to events was considered sufficient.

The government fully recognizes the need to improve the statistical services, and it is planned to increase both their coverage and depth over the rest of the decade.

Bibliography

Abusada R. *Propiedad Social: Algunas Consideraciones Economicas.* C.I.S.E.P.A., Lima (1973).

Anaya E. *Imperialismo, Industrialización y Transferencia de Tecnología en el Perú*, Horizonte, Lima (1975).

Astiz C. *Pressure Groups and Power Politics in Peruvian Politics*, Cornell U.P. (1969).

Baran P. *The Political Economy of Growth*, MR Press, New York (1957).

Barraclough S. *Agrarian Structure in Latin America*, Heath, Lexington (1973).

B.C.R. Banco Central de Reserva *Plan Nacional de Desarrollo Economico y Social del Perú 1962–71*, Lima (1961).

B.C.R. *Cuentas Nacionales del Perú 1950–65*, Lima (1967).

B.C.R. *Cuentas Nacionales del Perú 1960–73*, Lima (1974a).

B.C.R. *El Desarrollo Economico y Financiero del Perú*, Lima (1974b).

B.C.R. *Boletin del Banco Central de Reserva*, Lima (Dec. 1974c).

Beaulne M. *La Industrialisación por Sustitución de Importaciones en el Perú 1958–69*, E.S.A.N., Lima (1974).

Bertram G. *Development Problems in an Export Economy: Domestic Capitalists, Foreign Firms and Government in Peru 1919–1930*, D.Phil. dissertation, Oxford (1974).

Bourricaud F. *Power and Society in Contemporary Peru*, Faber, London (1970).

Carlson J. *Peru's and Colombia's Policies on Private Foreign Investment and Foreign Technology*, I.D.R., Copenhagen (1974).

C.D.E.S. Centro de Documentacion Economico-Social *Las Empresas Estatales*, Lima (1965).

C.E.M.L.A. Centro de Estudios Monetarios Latino-Americanos *El Mercado de Capitales en el Perú*, Mexico (1968).

Cibotti R. & Sierra E. *El Sector Publico en la Planificación del Desarrollo*, Siglo XXI, Mexico (1970).

C.N.S.E.V. Comisión Nacional Supervisora de Empresas y Valores *Flujo de Fondos Financieros en el Peru* 1965–1970, Lima (1973).

Coutu A. & King R.A. *The Agricultural Development of Peru*, Praegar, N.Y. (1969).

Delgado C. *El Proceso Revolucionario Peruano*, Siglo XXI, Mexico (1972).

E.C.L.A. Economic Commission for Latin America. *The Distribution of Income in Latin America*. Econ.Bull.Lat.Amer.Vol.XII.2 (1967).

E.C.L.A. *Planning and Plan Implementation in Latin America*, Econ.Bull.Lat.Amer., XIV.2 (1967).

E.C.L.A. *Public Enterprises: their Present Significance and their Potential in Development*, Econ.Bull.Lat.Amer., XVI.1 (1971a).

E.C.L.A. *Economic Survey of Latin America; 1969*, Santiago (1971b).

Espinoza H. *Dependencia Económica y Tecnológica*, Villarreal U.P., Lima (1971).

Espinoza H. *et al El Poder Económico en la Industria*, Villarreal U.P., Lima (1972).

Fei J. & Ranis G. *Development of the Labour Surplus Economy*, Irwin, N.Y. (1964).

Fitzgerald E.V.K. *The Public Sector in Latin America*, Centre of Latinamerican Studies Working Paper No.18, Cambridge (1974).

Fitzgerald E.V.K. *Some Aspects of Industrialisation in Peru 1965–75*, Centre of Latinamerican Studies Working Paper No.24, Cambridge (1975).

Fitzgerald E.V.K. *The Urban Service Sector, the Supply of Wagegoods and the Shadow Wage Rate*, Oxford Economic Papers, March (1976).
Frankman M.J. *Sectoral Policy Preferences of the Peruvian Government 1946–68*, Jour.Lat. Amer.Stud. (Nov. 1974).
Furtado C. *Economic Development of Latin America*, Cambridge U.P., (1970).
Gerschenkron A. *Economic Backwardness in Historical Perspective*, Harvard U.P. (1966).
Goodsell C.T. *American Corporations and Peruvian Politics*, Harvard U.P. (1974).
Griffin K. (ed.) *Financing Development in Latin America*, Macmillan, London (1971).
Griffin K. *The Political Economy of Agrarian Change*, Macmillan, London (1974).
Griffin K. & Enos J.L. *Planning Development*, Addison, London (1972).
Hanson A.H. *Public Enterprise and Economic Development*, Routledge, London (1965).
Harberger A.C. *La Tasa de Rendimiento en Colombia*, Revist.Plan.y Des., Bogota (Oct. 1969).
Harding C. *Agrarian Reform and Agrarian Struggles in Peru*, Centure of L.A. Studies, Cambridge (1974).
Haya de la Torre V. *El Plan de Acción*, Ed.Pueblo, Lima (1961).
Horton D. *Land Reform and Reform Enterprises in Peru*, Land Tenure Centre, Wisconsin (1974).
Hunt S. *Distribution, Growth and Government Economic Behaviour in Peru*, in Ranis G. (ed.) 'Government and Economic Development', Yale U.P. (1971).
Hunt S. *Direct Foreign Investment in Peru: New Rules for an Old Game*, Wilson School, Princeton (1974).
Ingram G.M. *Expropriation of U.S. Property in Latin America*, Praeger, N.Y. (1974).
I.N.P. Instituto Nacional de Planificación *Plan de Desarrollo Economico y Social 1967–70*, Lima (1967).
I.N.P. *Plan del Perú 1971–75*, Lima (1971).
I.N.P. *La Planificación Peruana*, Lima (1972a).
I.N.P. *La Administración de la Planificación Peruana*, Lima (1972b).
I.N.P. *Proyecciones a Largo Plazo de la Población y de la Economía del Perú*, Lima (1973a).
I.N.P. *Evaluación del Presupuesto de Inversión del Sector Público 1971–72*, Lima (1973b).
I.N.P. *Relaciones Inter-industriales de la Economía Peruana: Tabla Insumo-Producto 1969*, Lima (1973c).
I.N.P. *Modelo de Simulacion INP–1*, Lima (1973d).
I.N.P. *Estudio sobre la Población Peruana*, Lima (1974a).
I.N.P. *Evaluación del Presupuesto de Inversión del Sector Público 1973*, Lima (1974b).
I.N.P. *Analisis Económico Financiero de las Empresas Públicas 1973*, Lima (1974c).
I.N.P. *Perú: Precio Social de la Divisa*, Lima (1975a).
I.N.P. *Plan Nacional de Desarrollo 1975–78*, Lima (1975b).
Kalecki M. *Problems of Financing Economic Development in a Mixed Economy*, (1972a) in 'Essays on the Economic Growth of the Socialist and the Mixed Economy', Cambridge U.P. (1972).
Kalecki M. *Social and Economic Aspects of Intermediate Regimes*, (1972b) in Kalecki *op.cit.*
Kilty J. *Planning in Peru*, Praeger, N.Y. (1967).
Levin J.V. *The Export Economies*, Harvard U.P. (1960).
Lewis W.A. *Economic Development with Unlimited Supplies of Labour*, Manchester School (1954).
Little I.M.D. & Mirrlees J.R. *Social Cost-benefit Analysis of Industrial Projects*, O.E.C.D. Paris (1968).
Llarena A. *La Comunidad Industrial*, Villarreal U.P., Lima (1972).
Mabro R. *The Egyptian Economy 1952–72*, Oxford U.P. (1972).
Malpica C. *El Mito de la Ayuda Exterior*, Moncloa, Lima (1972).
Malpica C. *Los Dueños del Perú*, Peisa, Lima (1974).
Mariategui J.C. *Siete Ensayos sobre la Realidad Peruana*, Lima (1927).
Marret R. *Peru*, Knight, London (1969).
Matos J. & Ravines R. *Bibliografia Peruana de Ciencias Sociales 1957–69*, Instituto de Estudios Peruanos, Lima (1971).

MinAg Ministerio de Agricultura *Metodología para Dar Prioridad Sectorial a los Proyectos de Inversion*, Lima (1972).
MinAg *El Sector Agrario* (text of speech by Minister), Lima (1974).
Millones O. *La Oferta de los Productos Alimenticios a la Zona Urbana*, C.I.S.E.P.A., Lima (1973).
Millward R. *Public Expenditure Economics*, McGraw-Hill, London (1971).
Morawetz D. *The Andean Pact*, M.I.T. Press (1974).
O'Brien P. *The Revolution in Egypt's Economic System*, Oxford U.P. (1966).
O.N.E.C. Oficina Nacional de Estadistica y Censos *Anuario Estadistico – 1966*, Lima (1969).
O.N.E.C. *Anuario Estadistico – 1971*, Lima (1973).
O.N.E.C. *Precios al Por Mayor y al Por Menor*, Lima (1975).
Payne J.L. *Labor and Politics in Peru*, Yale U.P. (1965).
Payter C. *The Debt Trap*, Penguin, London (1974).
Petras J. & LaPorte R. *Perú: Transformación Revolucionaria o Modernización*, Amorrortu, B. Aires (1971).
Pike F.B. *The Modern History of Peru*, Praeger, N.Y. (1967).
Pinelo A.J. *The Multinational Corporation as a Force in Latin American Politics: a Case Study of the IPC*, Praeger, N.Y. (1973).
P.R.P. Presidencia de la Republica Peruana *Linamientos del Plan Nacional de Desarrollo para 1975–78*, Lima (1974).
Quijano A. *Nationalism and Capitalism in Peru*, M.R. Press, N.Y. (1971).
Roel V. *La Planificación Economica en el Perú*, Lima (1968).
Roemer M. *Fishing for Growth*, Harvard U.P. (1970).
Saberbein G. *Industrie et Sous-devéloppement au Perou*, Doctoral dissertation, Grenoble (1973).
Sachs I. *Patterns of Public Sector in Under-developed Economies*, Asia P.H., Bombay (1964).
Smith C. *The Regional Impact of Agrarian Reform in Peru*, Centre of L.A. Studies, Liverpool (1975).
Sunkel O. & Paz P. *El Subdesarrollo Latinoamericano y la Teoría des Desarrollo*, Siglo XXI, Mexico (1971).
Thorbeke E. & Condos A. *Macroeconomic Growth and Development Models of the Peruvian Economy* in Adelman I. and Thorbeke E. 'The Theory and Design of Economic Development' Johns Hopkins, N.Y. (1966).
Thorp R. *Inflation and Orthodox Economic Policy in Peru*, Bull.Ox.Inst.Econ.Stat. (Aug. 1967).
Thorp R. *Inflation and the Financing of Economic Development*, in Griffin *op.cit.* (1971).
Thorp R. *The Process of Industrialisation in Peru 1940–68*, Centre of L.A. Studies, Oxford (1975).
Torres J. *La Estructure de la Economía Peruana*, C.I.S.E.P.A., Lima (1974).
Twomey M. *Ensayos sobre la Agriculture Peruana*, C.I.S.E.P.A. (1973).
U.N.I.D.O. United Nations Industrial Development Organization *Manual on Economic Development Projects*, N.Y. (1958).
Villanueva V. *Cien Años del Militarismo en el Perú*, Baca, Lima (1971).
Waterson A. *Development Planning. the Lessons of Experience*, Oxford U.P. (1966).
Webb R.C. *Politica Tributaria e Incidencia de los Impuestos en el Perú*, U.Catolica, Lima (1972a).
Webb R.C. *The Distribution of Income in Peru*, Wilson School, Princeton (1972b).
Webb R.C. *Government Policy and Distribution of Income in Peru 1963–73*, Wilson School, Princeton (1973).
Zimmerman A. *El Plan Inca – Objetivo: Revolución Peruana*, El Peruano, Lima (1974).

75 21915